W9-ADA-416

"ALL LABOR HAS DIGNITY"

BOOKS BY MICHAEL K. HONEY

Southern Labor and Black Civil Rights:
Organizing Memphis Workers

Black Workers Remember:
An Oral History of Segregation, Unionism,
and the Freedom Struggle

Going Down Jericho Road:
The Memphis Strike, Martin Luther King's
Last Campaign

THE KING LEGACY

Stride Toward Freedom

"Thou, Dear God"

The Trumpet of Conscience

*Where Do We Go from Here:
Chaos or Community?*

Why We Can't Wait

© Walter P. Reuther Library, Wayne State University

African American women holding signs and wearing hats that show United Automobile Workers union support for civil rights stand in front of the White House during the March on Washington for Jobs and Freedom, August 28, 1963.

"ALL LABOR HAS DIGNITY"

MARTIN LUTHER KING, JR.

Edited with introductions by Michael K. Honey

BEACON PRESS
BOSTON

WILLARD LIBRARY, BATTLE CREEK, MI

BEACON PRESS
25 Beacon Street
Boston, Massachusetts 02108–2892

Beacon Press books are published under the auspices of the
Unitarian Universalist Association of Congregations.

No part of this book may be used or reproduced in any manner
whatsoever without written permission except in the case of brief
quotations embodied in critical articles and reviews.
For permission or for more information, contact
Writers House, 21 West 26th Street, New York, NY 10010.

"ALL LABOR HAS DIGNITY"
Copyright © 1963 by Martin Luther King, Jr.
Copyright © renewed 1986 by Coretta Scott King, Dexter King,
Martin Luther King III, Yolanda King, Bernice King. All rights reserved.

Introductions copyright © 2011 Michael K. Honey

Audio available at www.beacon.org/laborhasdignity

 In Association With **IPM**
INTELLECTUAL PROPERTIES
MANAGEMENT, INC.

Beacon Press gratefully acknowledges the
Unitarian Universalist Veatch Program at Shelter Rock
for its generous support of the King Legacy series.
Some spelling and punctuation have been adjusted, and
obvious errors have been corrected.

Printed in the United States of America

15 14 13 12   8 7 6 5 4 3 2 1

Text design by Wilsted & Taylor Publishing Services

Library of Congress Cataloging in Publication Data

King, Martin Luther, Jr., 1929–1968.
"All labor has dignity" / Martin Luther King, Jr. ; edited, with
introductions by Michael K. Honey.
p. cm.
Includes bibliographical references and index.
ISBN 978-0-8070-8602-5 (paperback : alk. paper)
1. Employee rights. 2. Social rights. 3. King, Martin Luther, Jr.,
1929–1968. I. Honey, Michael K. II. Title.
HD6971.8.K56 2011   331.01'1—dc22
2010033721

WILLARD LIBRARY, BATTLE CREEK, MI

Differences have been contrived . . . to impose disunity by dividing brothers because the color of their skin has a different shade. I look forward confidently to the day when all who work for a living will be one with no thought to their separateness as Negroes, Jews, Italians, or any other distinctions. This will be the day when we shall bring into full realization the American dream— a dream yet unfulfilled. A dream of equality of opportunity, of privilege and property widely distributed; a dream of a land where men will not take necessities from the many to give luxuries to the few, a dream of a land where men will not argue that the color of a man's skin determines the content of his character; a dream of a nation where all our gifts and resources are held not for ourselves alone but as instruments of service for the rest of humanity; the dream of a country where every man will respect the dignity and worth of human personality—that is the dream.

— MARTIN LUTHER KING, JR.
AFL-CIO National Convention, Miami Beach, Florida
December 11, 1961

CONTENTS

PART II
Standing at the Crossroads:
Race, Labor, War, and Poverty

PART III
Down Jericho Road:
The Poor People's Campaign and Memphis Strike

INTRODUCTION

*The two most dynamic and cohesive liberal forces
in the country are the labor movement and the
Negro freedom movement. Together we can be
architects of democracy.*

— MARTIN LUTHER KING, JR.,
at the AFL-CIO National Convention,
Miami Beach, Florida, December 11, 1961

During the last year of his life, Martin Luther King, Jr., put justice for poor and working-class people at the center of his agenda. He launched his Poor People's Campaign, demanding that Congress shift the country's spending from war to housing, health care, education, and jobs. He traveled the country in a whirlwind, scarcely sleeping, preaching the gospel of economic justice. Harking back to the nation's history of slavery and segregation, he demanded affirmative programs to overcome generations of denial and neglect for people once enslaved. But he didn't stop there. He sought an Economic Bill of Rights for Native Americans, Mexican Americans, Puerto Ricans, and poorer whites, as well as for blacks. He sought to create a nonviolent army of poor people in jobless inner cities and barrios and in reservations and rural areas. He challenged the country to create an economy of full employment, or lacking that, a tax system that ensured a decent level of income for every American.

King's exhausting schedule brought him to the brink of collapse. And yet when his colleague and friend James Lawson asked him to Memphis to support black sanitation workers on strike for union recognition, King went.

In Memphis, he renewed his faith in people's movements and found a powerful constituency of the working poor organized into a union-community alliance. In going to Memphis, King returned to an issue he had fought for all of his life: the right of working people to organize unions of their own choosing, free of employer harassment and police intimidation. Unions, he underscored, were the "first anti-poverty program" and they should be accessible to all who work for wages. Dignity for the working poor became another plank in his Poor People's Campaign.

King ultimately lost his life when an assassin cut him down in Memphis on April 4, 1968. Today, that awful murder often blots out the history of the Memphis movement, as well as King's struggle for the poor and working poor. Too many people still think of King in a narrow sense as a "civil rights" rather than as a human rights leader, losing sight of the breadth of the alliances and social movements he promoted. In contrast, union advocates remember King as a champion of labor rights, a working-class hero. Perhaps our own time of economic turmoil provides a moment in which we need to see King anew.

When most people imagine King, he's in a suit and tie at the Lincoln Memorial on August 28, 1963. King's glorious "Dream" speech plays on television and radio on King's birthday, often to the exclusion of some of his other important messages. Looking at the television images more closely, we might ask, Who are the men with the little white paper hats standing with such evident satisfaction behind King? On the podium and throughout King's vast audience one can see these union members, women and men with picket signs, buttons, and hats demanding "Fair Employment, Full Employment" and "Jobs and Freedom." These messages of solidarity were produced in the thousands by unions that also subsidized the public address system and chartered buses and planes that brought tens of thousands of trade unionists to the March on Washington.

United Automobile Workers (UAW) president Walter Reuther spoke from the podium calling for a "great moral crusade to arouse Americans to the unfinished work of democracy." John Lewis of the Student Nonviolent Coordinating Committee (SNCC) called for a revolution in southern race relations; Dorothy Height of the National Council of Negro Women and Rosa Parks stood with King on the podium; the elderly president of the Brotherhood of Sleeping Car Porters union, A. Philip Randolph, introduced King as "the moral leader of our nation."

Both civil rights and labor issues had been key to the mobilization. Black labor leader Cleveland Robinson, secretary-treasurer of District 65 of the Retail, Wholesale and Department Store Union (RWDSU) and vice president of the Negro American Labor Council (NALC), along with Randolph, had first proposed the march to pressure the American Federation of Labor and Congress of Industrial Organizations (AFL-CIO), a federation that included most labor unions, for stronger civil rights policies. Working with King and other civil rights leaders, they broadened their initial proposal into a March for Jobs and Freedom in order to focus the power of the mass movement rolling across the South on the federal government. Robinson served as treasurer while his union donated office space and salary for long-time activist Bayard Rustin to organize the March on Washington.

The AFL-CIO didn't endorse the march, but the federation's industrial union department and the UAW, both headed by Reuther, did. King's cultivation of an alliance between unions and the civil rights movement helped to spur the mass participation of unionists in the March on Washington. King spoke regularly to unions that had strong civil rights programs and large proportions of minority workers. From Montgomery to Memphis, King had consistently aligned himself with ordinary working people, supporting their demands for workplace rights and economic justice. His life did not so much illustrate the "great man" theory that heroic individuals are the prime movers of the historical process, but rather showed the power of people working in alliances and building social movements from the bottom up.

Throughout King's time of leadership, working-class and poor people and especially women played a major, if underestimated, role in the black freedom movement. Before the March on Washington came the spring 1963 mass movement in Birmingham, Alabama, in which over nine hundred young people went to jail and faced police dogs and fire hoses in an effort to desegregate that violent city. These sons and daughters of black steel workers, service workers, female domestic workers, and the city's small black middle class of preachers, teachers, and businesspeople fought to compete fairly for jobs, be treated as equals, and have the infamous "white" and "colored" signs taken down.

Similarly in Montgomery in 1956, for 381 days black female domestic workers, janitors, and others had refused to ride the buses. These working-class foot soldiers, especially women, walked or hitched rides to their jobs in order to bring segregation on the buses to an end. King is well known for helping to build campaigns for civil and voting rights populated by students, preachers, and the middle class, but in these key struggles he also demonstrated the powerful affinity he felt with poor and working people who propelled these movements.

As this book documents, northern-based unions provided significant political and financial support to the civil rights movement in the South. King turned to unions repeatedly for help, and in turn also helped the unions. As early as 1958, he spoke out against deceptively worded "right to work" laws, and in 1964, he helped to defeat such a proposal in Oklahoma that he said "provides no 'rights' and no 'work.'" In December 1963, he returned from accepting the Nobel Peace Prize in Oslo, Norway, to stand on picket lines with striking black women at the Scripto pen factory in Atlanta and then helped them to get a strike settlement in 1964. In 1965, King and the Southern Christian Leadership Conference (SCLC) considered training civil rights activists to be union organizers. King's prodding on issues of racism, poverty, and war also pushed many unionists to fuse their support for civil and labor rights into an even broader social justice agenda. In 1967, King keynoted a conference of unionists opposing the Vietnam War, opening a labor front for the peace movement.

Finally, in 1968, King fought to build the Poor People's Campaign and made explicit his commitment to work on behalf of unions to improve the conditions of the black working poor by going to Memphis. Declaring that "all labor has dignity," King stated that sanitation workers deserved a living wage and union rights, for what made labor menial was not hard and dirty work, but lack of union rights and poor conditions. As he told the Local 1199 hospital workers union a short while before he came to Memphis, "You see, no labor is really menial unless you're not getting adequate wages."

The civil rights and labor movements truly joined forces in Memphis. King perished in the struggle for union rights, but in large part due to his sacrifice, Local 1733 of the American Federation of State, County and Municipal Employees (AFSCME) won its strike. The victory in Memphis, though won at a great cost, gave added impetus to an organizing surge among public employees that made AFSCME into one of the largest unions in the country.

If in the past we have seen King primarily as a middle-class civil rights leader, it is now time to see him through the prism of his kinship to the poor, to working people, and to unions. From that perspective, we have much to learn about King and the movements of the 1960s.

While researching labor and civil rights history in 1992, I discovered a cache of King's speeches to unions in the archives at the Martin Luther King, Jr., Center for Nonviolent Social Change in Atlanta. Since then, I have chronicled the struggles of black and white workers to organize unions in the South and also tracked King's support for civil rights unionism in the searing battle in Memphis. But I continued to look back to these largely unknown speeches, trying to understand their context and significance. In these documents, King continually tried to connect the labor movement with the civil rights movement and to connect them both to broad efforts for social reform.

As part of Beacon Press's King Legacy series, this collection brings to light fifteen of King's speeches (and one non-speech document) relating to union rights and economic justice, twelve of them never before published in book form. Introductions provide details and context for the reader. These documents help us connect King's movement activity in Montgomery, Albany, Birmingham, Selma, Detroit, Chicago, New York, and Memphis to his evolving agenda for what he called "economic equality"—a belief that everyone be assured of a decent life in one of the richest countries in the world. King hoped for a future in which racism, poverty, and war would be relics of the past.

Other people had similar hopes and had struggled for years to transform them into reality. In this book, King constantly refers back to the American labor movement of the 1930s and links its sit-ins, sit-downs, picket lines, strikes, and boycotts to the civil rights battles of the 1960s. King saw the two movements as twin pillars of social progress in twentieth century America. But he wanted to go further, to create an ever more articulated, powerful labor and civil rights alliance.

King's kinship with the poor and his support for unions and economic fairness goes back to his youth and to his family's own struggle for an equal place at the American table. Born at the onset of the Great Depression, in 1929, King grew up in the striving black business district on Atlanta's Auburn Avenue. His father, "Daddy" King, protected Martin and his siblings and presented the model of a respectable, middle-class patriarch. Yet, in reality, the King family's experience was not far removed from poverty and labor exploitation. At least three of Martin's great-grandparents were slaves, and one of his grandfathers celebrated his birthday as January 2, 1863, the day after President Abraham Lincoln's Emancipation Proclamation took effect.

After emancipation, the Williams (on his mother's side) and King families worked on land owned by whites and spent most of their lives in debt. They lived difficult lives that offered neither the certainty of being fed and clothed, nor the true freedom to engage in economic, social, and political pursuits. Both men and women did hard labor. Delia Linsey, Martin's grandmother, worked for white folks, washing and ironing, trying to supplement the family's meager income as she and James King moved from place to place sharecropping and working for wages. King's grandfather, A. D. Williams, lost a thumb in a sawmill accident and moved to Atlanta, doing hard labor in order to escape lynching and labor exploitation in the countryside. King's father also escaped the plantation districts of Georgia, arriving in the city in 1913 with little but the clothes on his back.

King's family turned to the black church and the social gospel of Jesus to climb out of the poverty and demoralization of the Jim Crow system. "I am fundamentally a clergyman, a Baptist preacher," Martin explained in 1965. "This is my being and my heritage for I am also the son of a Baptist preacher, the grandson of a Baptist preacher, and the great-grandson of a Baptist preacher." In that same lineage, he was the descendant of slaves, sharecroppers, urban workers, and religious entrepreneurs. Both the men and the women in this lineage faced political, economic, and racial discrimination that kept them out of skilled jobs and blocked their educational opportunities.

As historian Clayborne Carson emphasizes, and the Martin Luther King, Jr., Research and Education Institute at Stanford University documents, the black Christian social gospel demanded that all of God's children should have equal rights. King's grandfather, A. D. Williams, and his wife, Jennie, and King's father, Michael King, and his wife, Alberta, built Ebenezer Baptist Church in Atlanta. From a tiny congregation, it became a powerhouse for civil rights and voting rights agitation that also took care of the social welfare of its congregants.

Coming from such a family, the young Martin Luther King, Jr., naturally empathized with the plight of poor and working-class people in the neighborhood surrounding his family home. In the 1930s, his father took him to see the unemployment lines, and although Martin later became critical of his father's materialism, he never forgot Daddy King's respect for the poor, a respect that King, Jr., also exhibited throughout his life.

The Great Depression further sensitized Martin to the gap between rich and poor and animated what he later called his "anti-capitalistic feelings." He witnessed people standing in bread lines and the effects of poverty within his father's congregation. As a teenager, he worked for a summer on a Connecticut tobacco farm and saw the damage that poverty and racial hatred did to poor whites as well as to blacks. In both the South as well as the North, what King later called the "malignant kinship" between race and class remained readily apparent.

In short, although King was indeed "middle class" in demeanor, his family heritage, his own experiences, and the black Christian social gospel also provided King with a life-long framework within which to demand justice for workers and the poor. King's college education also created an intellectual foundation for understanding these inequalities. At age fifteen, Martin entered Morehouse College in an accelerated program during World War II. As the U.S. pledged to fight fascism, racism, anti-Semitism, and colonialism, King was profoundly influenced through courses in sociology, history, philosophy, literature, and religion. Morehouse president Dr. Benjamin Mays (and others King later encountered) popularized Mahatma Gandhi's respect for the poor, highlighting his success in nonviolent organizing against colonialism, caste systems, and labor exploitation. Even as a young student, King began to fuse religion, academic knowledge, and his family's long-standing activism on behalf of equal rights and social justice.

King went on to graduate school at Crozer Theological Seminary and Boston University, but he had already joined a special generation of human rights activists. Black students and war veterans of the 1940s mainstreamed a more militant civil rights consciousness at a time when the U.S. government promised to overturn the old ways of imperialism and inequality throughout the world. It was a powerful time, what one historian called the "seedtime" of the black revolution. Organized labor played an essential part in undergirding that revolution. The 1935 Wagner Act had established the right to freedom of speech and the right to organize on the job for the first time in U.S. history. Millions of workers in steel, auto, meatpacking, electrical, rubber, and other basic industries joined unions under the banner of the Congress of Industrial Organizations (CIO). W. E. B. Du Bois, in 1944, saw this as a great turn of events and wrote that the CIO provided the best hope for equal rights in the postwar era.

Unfortunately, the vision of anti-colonial, liberationist struggles abroad and expanded union and civil rights at home got fractured by the great Red Scare of the post–World War II era. The Red Scare undermined both the civil rights movement and the American labor movement and constricted the broader vision for change wrought by the war. Some argue the U.S. government's anti-communist crusades of the late 1940s, 1950s, and 1960s provided additional leverage to demand full civil rights. King and others rightly said that if the U.S. wanted to be a global model of freedom, it would have to eliminate segregation at home. The strength of this argument and the need to get black votes in the urban North caused President Harry S. Truman to desegregate the U.S. armed forces and call for civil and political rights for African Americans. The U.S. Supreme Court also made this argument in its historic *Brown v. Board of Education* decision to overthrow segregation as the law of the land.

From the perspective of labor history, however, scholars increasingly recognize the damage done by the postwar Red Scare. At the height of the labor movement's power, when approximately a third of workers (and 50 percent of industrial workers) belonged to unions, the Red Scare's big squeeze against labor radicalism eliminated some of the most persistent and militant voices for interracial working-class mobilization. It also helped to block unions from expanding into difficult-to-organize areas of low-wage employment, where workers of color and women predominated. Operation Dixie, an effort begun by the CIO in 1946 to fully organize the workers of the South, might have created powerful union allies for civil rights reform. Instead, red-baiting, race-baiting, violence, and laws restricting the right to organize left the South a bastion of anti-unionism.

Without unions, African American, Mexican American, and Euro-American workers in the South lacked a means to improve their conditions at work or to build independent political power. As is apparent from his speeches in part 1 of this book, King clearly understood the importance of unionizing the South. He saw it as a way to elevate wages, enfranchise African Americans and workers, and to vote more labor-friendly and less racist people into power. He particularly wanted to remove the "Neanderthals" in the U.S. Senate who used the filibuster to block all significant change. He believed the unions and civil rights forces together could push history in a better direction. The Knights of Labor, the Industrial Workers of the World, the United Mine Workers, and many industrial unions had at times followed a path of interracial labor solidarity, and left a promising history of labor-based social change.

But King also knew that the American union movement had a contradictory, dual character regarding racial minorities and women. If the CIO offered hope to black workers and women, building trades unions and brotherhoods of railroad workers in the older American Federation of Labor (AFL) still largely excluded or segregated minority and women workers. The National Labor Relations Board (NLRB) did not require unions using its services to ban union discrimination. Even blacks in unionized industries still experienced exclusionary union and apprenticeship programs, segregated locals and workplaces, and outright violence and bigotry at the hands of white workers. And supposedly progressive CIO unions often codified discriminatory job assignments and seniority lines in their contracts, despite equal rights provisions in their own constitutions.

From the 1930s onward, Communists and assorted non-aligned labor radicals had fought segregationist practices at work and in society, and led the way in organizing women and men into unions across color and gender barriers. But especially after the war, labor radicals fought their way upstream against a torrent of institutionalized racism and Cold War anti-communism. The Republican-dominated Congress elected in 1946 imposed the Taft-Hartley Act of 1947, which amended the Wagner Act to force union leaders to swear they were not Communists or lose federal election supervision protections through the NLRB. Taft-Hartley tied up unions in legal bureaucracy and fatally weakened them by allowing states to ban the union shop, thus allowing workers to benefit from a union contract without joining the union. Taft-Hartley also restricted union political action and undermined organizing in various other ways.

CIO unions initially resisted Taft-Hartley and disliked Democratic president Harry S. Truman, whose loyalty-security and anti-communist foreign policies helped start the Cold War and the Red Scare. But during the presidential election of 1948, the CIO grew desperate for unity and required all of its member unions to support Truman. After union votes sealed Truman's victory, the CIO expelled its eleven supposedly Communist-led unions with nearly one million members that had supported Progressive Party presidential candidate Henry Wallace, who advocated détente with the Soviet Union. Disagreements over U.S. foreign policy thus polarized the CIO. Although unions went on to reach their high point of institutional power, hard-line anti-communism would divide many of the unions from King and the burgeoning movements of the 1960s.

Organized labor from 1949 on presented a confusing picture to civil rights advocates such as King. On one hand, unions made substantial contract gains and became key political players that helped to establish the basis for the Great Society and civil rights victories of the 1960s. Conversely, the CIO expelled some of its strongest civil rights unionists in the South and raided major unions such as the United Electrical, Radio and Machine Workers Union (UE) for following the "Communist Party line."

These matters might seem somewhat removed from the civil rights struggle, but they would have momentous consequences for King's attempt to build a labor–civil rights alliance. In 1955, CIO and AFL unions merged to create a larger, stronger federation, but because the CIO had five million members and the AFL had twice that many (and because the CIO was on the verge of disintegration), the more racially conservative AFL took the greater share of leadership. Many unions became more bureaucratic, top-down institutions. The Red Scare also tied the AFL-CIO to a U.S. foreign policy establishment that King came to oppose.

Tragically, led by President George Meany and International Affairs Director Jay Lovestone, the AFL-CIO aggressively supported the U.S. as it abrogated elections scheduled for 1956 in Vietnam and supported a string of corrupt governments hated by their own people. Lovestone worked with the CIA in undermining leftist unions in Europe and in overthrowing nationalist governments in poor countries such as Guatemala (the CIA also helped to overthrow an elected government in Iran, leading to generations of conflict). The AFL-CIO became the government's strongest foreign policy supporter and condemned those who opposed military intervention as unwitting dupes of supposed Communists.

As the Red Scare undermined international and inter-racial labor solidarity, the Montgomery Bus Boycott introduced the world to King and King to the world of civil rights unionism. There he found his strongest allies in black and left-led unions in and outside of the AFL-CIO.

King's relationship with unions began in Montgomery in December 1955, when King unleashed his extraordinary power to use the spoken word to evoke feelings of unity and determination to overcome frightful barriers to change. President A. Philip Randolph and local president E. D. Nixon of the Brotherhood of Sleeping Car Porters union approached other unions for financial support. Soon King began speaking, raising funds, and garnering political support from unions for the freedom movement in the South. Union support for the bus boycott cemented King's belief in their importance in building a cohesive national force for social change.

One of the CIO's left-led unions, the United Packinghouse Workers of America (UPWA) in the 1950s had the strongest union program for civil rights in the country. Even before the bus boycott, twenty-six members of an Atlanta local of the UPWA went to jail for protesting bus segregation. UPWA members had already faced down racists who tried to prevent housing integration in the Chicago area, and raised funds and protested on behalf of Mamie Bradley, the mother of Emmett Till, a black teenager murdered by racists in Mississippi on August 28, 1955. The UPWA refused to sign contracts unless they had an anti-discrimination clause and insisted that employers promote African Americans, Mexican Americans, and women to all levels of work and management in the packinghouses.

Three months into the Montgomery boycott, King met with UPWA activists in Chicago to plot strategy. The union threatened the company that owned the Montgomery bus system with a national boycott and raised a Fund for Democracy, not by fiat by the union's officers, but by a fund-raising campaign among its members. Black women, such as Addie Wyatt, became especially active in civil rights, and workers at the Chicago Armour meatpacking plant held a prayer vigil in support of the Montgomery campaign. After its triumph, black UPWA leaders Russell Lasley, John Henry Hall, and Charles Hayes attended the founding conference of King's SCLC. Lasley and Hayes served on its board along with District 65 black leader Cleveland Robinson.

All of this demonstrated to King the power of a national union network. Soon, he began working with the United Automobile Workers union and other unions that had significant black membership and supported civil rights. These included District 65 and Local 1199, both associated with the Retail, Wholesale and Department Store Employees Union (RWDSU). These unions tenaciously organized African American, Puerto Rican, and other Hispanic workers in the expanding service and health-care industries in New York City. Jewish labor radicals with roots in the 1930s thus helped to create two unions that, in the 1960s, became important supporters of King's civil rights movement in the South. District 65 and Local 1199 also became powerful sources of civil rights unionism in New York City itself.

Unions turned to building alliances with A. Philip Randolph, King, and the National Association for the Advancement of Colored People (NAACP). District 65— with strong leadership from Jamaican-born Cleveland Robinson, its secretary-treasurer and leader of its Negro Affairs Committee—organized New York City minority workers in department stores and various service industries. It set up picket lines and rallies supporting the civil rights movement, and, in 1959, Robinson and Randolph organized the NALC to pressure the AFL-CIO to attack racism within its ranks. In association with RWDSU and District 65, Local 1199 also attacked sub-minimum wages, high rents, and restrictive racial hiring. Black and Puerto Rican women in hospital employment became especially active in Local 1199. As Local 1199 president Leon Davis put it, "This is more than just another union; this is part of the freedom struggle."

This was the kind of labor movement King so desperately needed to build the labor–civil rights coalition in northern cities. King spoke repeatedly at District 65 and Local 1199 meetings, and King also found a home within the West Coast's International Longshore and Warehouse Union (ILWU). In 1963, ILWU president Harry Bridges threatened to refuse to load ships with goods made in Alabama in support of King's battles there. Bridges, an Australian seaman and longshoreman, fought and defeated federal government attempts to deport him as an "alien" Marxist for twenty years. He became a naturalized citizen, a fierce equal rights supporter (he broke the West's anti-miscegenation laws by marrying Japanese American Noriko "Nikki" Sawada), and a leading opponent of the American war in Vietnam. Black longshore workers in San Francisco's Local 10 welcomed him to speak there in 1967 as part of the ILWU family.

At the Labor Leaders Assembly for Peace in November 1967, King's allies in District 65, Local 1199, the UE, the UPWA, and the ILWU provided strong civil rights and peace advocates. King said he felt himself an honorary member of many unions, and, indeed, many of them had given him awards for his civil rights leadership. King's leftist union associations had helped him to develop an experiment in labor–civil rights solidarity that lasted until his death.

———◇◇◇———

In part 1 of this collection, the difficulties and contradictions of building labor–civil rights alliances in the shadow
of Cold War anti-communism can be seen in King's
speeches. King's Christian social gospel vision proved popular with union members, yet he also followed a pragmatic
agenda. Many of his early labor speeches are straight-out
appeals for funds and support in which he outlines the
triumphs and tragedies of the freedom movement. His
early speeches to the Highlander Folk School (previously
a meeting place for CIO organizers) and the UAW suggest a
perhaps unfounded optimism and hope for an easy alliance of progressive forces to change the politics and
priorities of the country. Yet his Highlander speech also
set off a segregationist campaign that depicted the Highlander meeting as a "Communist training school." From
that time forward the FBI and the American right wing
perpetually portrayed King as a Marxist-Leninist deceiver.

King's speeches in part 1 cover the highlights of the
movement he is associated with: the Montgomery Bus
Boycott; the student sit-ins and freedom rides; the Albany
and Birmingham movements for desegregation and the
hiring of black workers; the mass march in Detroit leading to the March on Washington in 1963; civil rights and
labor lobbying that led to the 1964 Civil Rights Act;
and the Selma to Montgomery march that led to the 1965
Voting Rights Act.

King's main goal was to garner financial and political
support for the southern movement, but he also developed
a second objective: supporting efforts by his labor allies
to fully desegregate unions and bring people of color into
union leadership. King was advised by Randolph, Robinson, Rustin, and others who knew the labor movement
better than he did, and they helped to shape his speeches

and approach to unions. (Among these advisors, former Communists with strong labor perspectives Stanley Levison and Hunter Pitts (Jack) O'Dell became special targets of the FBI and the White House.)

Others who could have been helpful to King in developing his perspective in his labor speeches might also have included Ralph Helstein, UPWA president, and black leaders of the UPWA in Chicago, as well as President Reuther and others in the UAW in Detroit. Levison counseled King on his 1961 AFL-CIO speech and King incorporated some of the text from his last book, 1967's *Where Do We Go From Here: Chaos or Community?*, in his last speeches to Local 1199 and the Teamsters in New York City in 1968.

In his speeches, King did not shrink from criticizing unions when they failed to eliminate racism and discrimination within their own ranks. Even as King repeatedly declared that a history of struggle had created a special relationship of solidarity between blacks and unions, he also insisted that this special relationship required a frank discussion of weaknesses as well as strengths.

King's address to the AFL-CIO in 1961 proved especially prescient. He argued that the "duality of interests of labor and Negroes" made them natural allies. But he also sharply criticized the federation for not going far enough to eliminate union racism and discrimination and for its efforts to silence the critical voice of A. Philip Randolph, who asked why unions could purge reds but not racists. "Negroes are almost entirely a working people. Our needs are identical with labor's needs," King declared. Yet he also warned of impending disaster if organized labor did not discard its racial and political conservatism to create a center-left political movement.

Prophetically, he warned that an "ultra-right wing" alliance, including "big military and big industry," and a reactionary grouping of southern Democrats and northern Republicans in Congress "now threaten everything decent and fair in American life." With automation grinding factory jobs into dust, King warned, "This period is made to order for those who would seek to drive labor into impotency." He urged unions to stop worrying about "scattered reds" and pay attention to the gathering storm of the center-right alliance trying to wipe them out.

Among the more leftist-led unions, King also moved beyond civil rights to the deeper and thornier problems of racial-economic inequality and war, telling a District 65 meeting in 1962 that "the evil of war, the evil of economic injustice, and the evil of racial injustice" were all intertwined. Such concerns are readily apparent in his speeches in part 11, which encompass a period when King's agenda shifted from attaining civil rights to creating a basis for "economic equality." Fortunately, organized labor provided a critical force to push the Civil Rights and Voting Rights acts of 1964 and 1965 through Congress. Federal laws now made employer and union-employment discrimination on the basis of race and sex illegal, and made it possible to register black voters to build the kind of labor–civil rights alliance King had long sought. But as soon as these victories sealed "phase one" of the civil rights movement, a new challenge arose. After the violent 1965 inner-city upheaval in Los Angeles called the Watts Riot, a sense of dire emergency increasingly animated King, who felt he had failed to fully address the problems of the poor and urban workers beyond the South. "The explosion in Watts reminded us all that the northern ghettos are the prisons of forgotten men," King wrote in a speech prepared for a District 65 convention in September 1965.

From this point on, King called for a "phase two" of the black freedom movement that would move beyond civil rights and voting rights to "economic equality." He asked unions to step to the forefront in the reordering of the nation's priorities to benefit ordinary people. In 1966, King went to Chicago (with help from the UAW and the UPWA) to organize a mass movement against institutionalized racism and poverty, and he marched against fear in Mississippi with Stokely Carmichael. But in both of these struggles King came away with very little to claim as victories. As the Vietnam War escalated and unemployed inner-city youth revolted, "black power" became the dominant rhetoric of black liberation portrayed in the mass media. King embraced the call for black power as legitimate, but he also felt increasing despair over the violent direction in which the country seemed to be heading and searched for a framework to create a new kind of coalition for change.

In 1967 and 1968, it seemed the country was at a crossroads and would either move forward toward more fundamental transformation or become increasingly embroiled in conflict over unresolved problems. In part III, King speaks in a prophetic voice of "two Americas," one composed of the rich and well-off, the other of poor people with little hope living on "a lonely island of poverty" in the midst of a seemingly affluent society. In a biting, critical, and prophetic commentary about the failure of American-style racial capitalism, he reminded his labor audiences that African Americans began in the chains of slavery and through their unpaid labor made cotton the king of the economy. But capital subsequently mechanized agricultural and industrial production and discarded their labor while increasingly moving unskilled factory employment to cheaper facilities abroad.

King had always called on his country to live up to the creed that "all men are created equal," with inalienable rights to "life, liberty, and the pursuit of happiness." But he now asked America to go beyond formal rights in the law to substantive forms of economic justice: jobs, health care, education, housing, and a hand up for those on the bottom of society. Although many whites had supported a "phase one" for civil and voting rights, King complained that they rejected a "phase two" demand for "economic equality." King warned that in order to remain relevant, the labor movement needed to become more radical and build alliances with poor and working-class communities beyond the workplace.

By 1967, King found himself at polar opposites from many national union leaders. At the National Labor Leadership Assembly for Peace in November, he expressed the hope that unions would reject militarism and become a part of the peace movement and what he called "forward-looking" America. He described Congress as "single-mindedly devoted to the pursuit of war" but "emotionally hostile to the needs of the poor." King now openly opposed a war in Vietnam that many union leaders supported. The UAW's international affairs director, Victor Reuther, Walter Reuther's brother, had already exposed the AFL-CIO's ties with the CIA. The West Coast ILWU leader Harry Bridges called U.S. policies, supported by most unions, "American imperialism with a union label." Although the peace assembly spurred King's call for a broader alliance of peace, labor, and civil rights organizations, the AFL-CIO seventh annual convention that followed it in Miami Beach fully embraced the war. King's hopes seemed to be "blowing in the wind."

Not only did King's anti-war position alienate him from many union leaders, but his economic analysis exceeded where most of them were willing to go. As he had said in his famous speech at Riverside Church in New York on April 4, 1967, against the Vietnam War, "When machines and computers and profit motives and property rights are considered more important than people, the giant triplets of racism, materialism, and militarism are incapable of being conquered." Unfortunately, King implied, that's the nation America may have become. He now placed his demands for economic justice in the context of a plea for a "moral revolution" to "shift from a 'thing-oriented' society to a 'person-oriented' society."

In 1968, King tried to move his economic agenda forward. In a speech to New York City's Local 1199 on March 10, King explained the need for a more transformative movement. He demanded a sharp reversal in American priorities by shifting money from bombs and war to health care, jobs, housing, and education. He said the U.S. had the wealth to eliminate poverty in the world but lacked the will to do it. He proposed to generate that will in a movement of the poor. King in previous statements had already told reporters he was "going for broke," in what he called the Poor People's Campaign.

In the middle of his mobilization to take poor people to Washington, King went to Memphis and reemphasized his belief that organized labor could move mountains when joined to a community-based movement. AFSCME national president Jerry Wurf and organizers William Lucy, Jesse Epps, and Joe Paisley worked in the trenches throughout the strike. As women mounted a boycott of downtown businesses, and raised funds and collected food to keep the strike alive, black ministers led by James Lawson mobilized the community through the black church. The workers' movement in Memphis escalated stunningly, but so did blunt resistance from a paternalistic, condescending, and ferociously anti-union mayor, Henry Loeb. The city's intransigence and violent police attacks on marchers changed a strike into a racial issue.

In the heart of the Mississippi cotton economy, Memphis exemplified the historic racial-economic system that

King said must be changed. In Memphis, 80 percent of African Americans, women as well as men, remained stuck in unskilled jobs at the bottom of the economy. The sanitation workers' strike for union rights threatened the racial pattern of white supremacy as well as a low-wage system based on cheap black labor. It was a classic civil rights strike, bringing together many of the issues King sought to address in the Poor People's Campaign. King told AFSCME workers and their supporters in Memphis on March 18 that the lowly sanitation worker is as important to the community's health as the doctor— literally true in a town nearly wiped out by yellow fever plagues after the Civil War for lack of an efficient public sanitation system. King's ability to merge moral and religious philosophy with labor and human rights issues illustrated once again why people constantly called on him to join their struggles.

"All labor has dignity," King reminded the workers and their supporters.

King's speeches to unions might help us to more fully appreciate the significance of King's connection to labor issues and to working-class people as part of his broad and unfinished agenda for human rights. If he were alive today, perhaps King would again be called a Communist for pursuing his Christian social gospel campaign for "economic justice." These previously unavailable speeches may help people in the current explosion of unemployment, homelessness, hunger, poverty, and war to think anew about issues that bedevil us today: continuing racial division and the politics of hate; machines and corporations taking people's jobs away; senators who filibuster to stop social progress; the waste of economic resources on failed military solutions to human problems; a widespread business-promoted culture of opposition to unions; and a mass media that fails to examine the intertwined destructive effects of racism, poverty, and war.

The destructive effects of deindustrialization and union decline on workers in places such as Detroit and Memphis cause King's speeches to resonate powerfully in our own times. Our purpose in publishing them is to fully bring back the legacy of King and the alliance for labor rights and economic justice that he tried to create. King's labor speeches will thus help us to deepen our understanding of the King era as one part of the longest of movements, the struggle for working people to live a decent life.

King's last two unscripted and poetic speeches in Memphis suggest that King's links to worker struggles for labor rights lay deep within his Christian philosophy and stretched back over a lifetime. King said the Constitution provided no guarantees but that the Declaration of Independence implied a promise of economic justice. "If a man does not have a job or an income, at that moment you deprive him of life. You deprive him of liberty. And you deprive him of the pursuit of happiness," he declared on March 18.

King also preached the power of "dangerous unselfishness" on the night before his death, on April 3, asking us to risk ourselves for the good of others as we travel down life's perilous Jericho Road. He asked everyone to be a Good Samaritan.

King preached in Memphis, "Either we go up together, or we go down together." Perhaps it is not yet too late to look over the mountaintop and see the promised land.

EDITOR'S NOTE

Two types of documents were used in this collection. One consists of speeches transcribed from tape recordings by people associated with King during his lifetime or shortly after his death, particularly by his book agent, Joan Daves. Often, such a transcript from a King audio, such as King's last two speeches in Memphis, provides the only version we have.

The other kind of document is a typed or partially handwritten (often in King's hand) text of a speech as King planned to deliver it. Sometimes scholars can verify how that speech was given through an audio recording and make corrections to the transcript.

In some cases, however, it is impossible to know whether King delivered all or only part of a speech, or in what order the words were delivered. For example, District 65, at that time affiliated to the Retail, Wholesale and Department Store Union (RWDSU), reproduced two of King's speeches on a heavily edited record that did not match the typed speech I found in the King archive in Atlanta. I relied upon the printed text and used the audio to verify or add to parts of it, since King clearly delivered more of the speech than is in the audio version. In such cases, I present the speech the way it appears King gave it.

In all cases, I verified speeches through recordings when we could find them, and researchers at Beacon took great care to correct the typed versions that we have been able to locate. In some cases, original transcripts noted crowd response, and we have also included crowd response when reviewing audio tapes and adding our own revisions to speeches. In other cases we had only a text and not a recording and so no crowd response is noted.

Through careful listening to the audio versions we could find and comparing them to written texts, we have produced what we think are the most accurate and complete versions of these speeches. I verified both transcribed audio and typed texts through union newspapers and secondary sources and draw my sometimes lengthy introductions from that same material. (See details in the appendix.)

I found two King labor speeches that others delivered on his behalf, including one given at the United Electrical, Radio and Machine Workers Union (UE) convention in 1962, which I did not think especially significant and therefore excluded from the collection. In the case of the convention of District 65, on September 18, 1965, King's representative, Andrew Young, gave a completely different speech from the one King had written, but King's written text was very significant and so is included in this collection.

As a rule, I intervened as little as possible in these speeches. Transcribers of King's recordings or typists of his original speech texts sometimes introduced minor typing errors, and I silently omitted these and removed other minor errors of spelling, syntax, or grammar, or illegible sections. In a few cases, I also removed text that repeats material from an earlier speech. King gave speeches constantly, so he frequently repeated certain phrases and themes, but repeating them in a written collection does not seem necessary or helpful to the reader. I have tried, however, not to remove material that would undermine the rhythm or content of the speech. All deletions in the text are marked with ellipses (. . .). In a few cases, I have inserted the full names or identification of people mentioned in King's speeches or added a word for clarification. All such editorial insertions are shown in brackets ([ ]). Any text shown in parentheses, except for audience response, existed in the original document.

Reading and hearing King's speeches are two different experiences. For that reason, we include with this book audio from two of King's speeches. Please note that the two audios accompanying this volume are incomplete. For that reason, they will not be identical to the text, particularly in the case of "The Unresolved Race Question." Please refer to the appendix for more information. The listener will immediately notice how King's inflections and the crowds' responses make his speeches come alive. His speech to District 65 in 1962 and his March 18, 1968, speech in Memphis demonstrate King's ability to capture important ideas that move an audience to action.

© Joseph Chapman

King speaking during "phase one" of the civil rights movement at the 16th Street Baptist Church in Birmingham, Alabama, sometime before Ku Klux Klan members bombed it on September 15, 1963.

PART I

Forging a Civil Rights–Labor Alliance in the Shadow of the Cold War

I still believe that organized labor can be one of the most powerful instruments to do away with this evil that confronts our nation that we refer to as segregation and discrimination. It is certainly true that the forces that are anti-Negro are by and large anti-labor, and with the coming together of the powerful influence of labor and all people of goodwill in the struggle for freedom and human dignity, I can assure you that we have a powerful instrument.

—"The Future of Integration," speech to the United Packinghouse Workers of America, AFL-CIO, Chicago, Illinois, October 2, 1957

I

"A look to the future"

I n 1931 and 1932, in the Cumberland Mountain plateau
of Tennessee, Myles Horton, James Dombrowski, and
Don West—white social gospel advocates involved with
communist and socialist politics and working-class movements of the Depression decade—created Highlander
Folk School on donated land in a little place called Monteagle. They followed a model of education through dia-
logue that presumed people could come up with solutions
to their own problems.

Highlander provided one of the few places in the South
where union activists could meet without threat of violent
attacks. The school helped foster a remarkable resurgence
of labor activism and helped wood, mine, packinghouse,
auto, and other workers to organize themselves. Highlander eschewed party labels but associated itself with the
major reforms of the New Deal. Labor organizing accelerated after Congress passed the National Labor Relations
Act (or Wagner Act) in 1935, for the first time protecting
civil rights and liberties at the workplace. Highlander's
leaders created an educational program to teach people
about labor history and the philosophy and tactics of
organizing and supported a new union movement. Ulti-

mately, the Congress of Industrial Organizations (CIO) emerged. Unlike most of the older unions in the American Federation of Labor (AFL) that were organized along craft lines, the new industrial unions organized all workers in an industry into a single unit regardless of race, ethnicity, gender, or political beliefs.

After World War II, Highlander disregarded all segregation laws and practices. A photo at the school in 1948 pictured whites and blacks "living . . . playing . . . and working together." Workshop participants ate at the same tables, slept in the same dormitories, talked, sang, swam, and even danced together without racial distinction. Rather than merely talking about integration, Highlander practiced it; whites uncomfortable with the practice had the choice of staying or leaving. After fighting an anti-fascist war in which African Americans served as soldiers and sailors and migrated in the millions into northern urban settings and mass production plants, many felt Jim Crow must go. The federal government began to integrate the armed forces and to support equal employment opportunity. Segregationist whites mounted a counteroffensive deriding those who tried to integrate society as Communists and race-mixers.

In the great Red Scare after the war, Highlander came under attack for supporting both labor organizing and integration. Bending to the Red Scare, the CIO tried to force Highlander to exclude workers and unions charged with being Communists. But Horton pointed out that leftist unions brought some of the most integrated delegations to the school; the CIO ban would eliminate black workers at the very time Highlander wanted to encourage them to use its facilities. The school also refused to discriminate against people for their political viewpoint, and the CIO cut off its funding to the school.

Subsequently, vigilantes, local police, and the state

of Tennessee tried to destroy Highlander. In 1959, Mississippi senator James Eastland, one of the Democratic Party's most racially bigoted and senior members, subpoenaed Horton to appear before his Senate Internal Security Subcommittee (SISS). He smeared Highlander's leaders as Communists while a Nashville Banner cartoon showed the school as a rotten tree surrounded by the words "racial agitation," "questionable activities," and "Commie front." In 1961, the state padlocked Highlander's doors, forcing it to move deeper into the mountains of eastern Tennessee.

In the 1950s, Highlander shifted its emphasis from labor organizing to supporting the burgeoning civil rights movement. In 1955, the school hosted Rosa Parks only weeks before she set off the Montgomery Bus Boycott by refusing to relinquish her seat to a white man. In 1957, Horton invited Dr. King to keynote Highlander's twenty-fifth anniversary, which Parks also attended. King opposed Communism on moral and philosophical grounds, but he believed every person had a right to his or her own opinions. During the Red Scare years, he signed petitions against the persecution of known or purported Communists, and he surely knew that speaking at Highlander meant he, too, would be attacked as a subversive. But he also knew that segregationists labeled as communist virtually anyone who supported civil rights. King did not hesitate to speak at Highlander.

In this speech, King looked at three historic periods of American race relations and optimistically charted a future in which southerners, white and black, would unite to replace segregation with a more open and humane social system. He viewed industrialization as a force for change and said "organized labor is one of the Negro's strongest allies in the struggle for freedom." He denounced White Citizens' Councils' efforts to recruit southern white workers into segregated units that threatened to "secede" from the national unions. On the basis of the U.S. Supreme Court's Brown v. Board of Education ruling, King fully expected integration to materialize, as well as industrialization, unionization, and expanded black voting rights that would produce more enlightened elected officials.

Asking people to rebel in an era of conformity, King challenged participants at the Highlander anniversary to be "maladjusted" to "the tragic inequalities of an economic system which takes necessities from the masses to give luxuries to the classes." King had long felt that capitalism as it existed in the U.S. was inequitable and had perpetuated racial division. Opposing Cold War orthodoxy, he declared, "I never intend to become adjusted to the madness of militarism and the self-defeating method of physical violence." King predicted that southern segregation would die because it was a liability to the United States as it promoted itself as a democratic alternative to the Soviet Union.

Singer Pete Seeger led participants in a rousing version of "We Shall Overcome," a song that Highlander's late music director Zilphia Horton had learned from black women strikers in Charleston, South Carolina, in 1947. As King drove away from Highlander with two of the South's most persecuted white radicals, Anne Braden of Louisville and W. E. "Red" Davis of St. Louis, he mused, "That song really stays with you, doesn't it?" The Highlander gathering lifted King's spirits immensely, yet his prediction of steady progress proved far too optimistic. His predictions relied heavily on the progress of organized labor, but in the years to come, hard-line anti-unionism battered southern workers. "Freedom of choice" and "right to work" rhetoric and laws enabled by section 14(b) of the Taft-Hartley Act outlawed the union shop, wherein all members of a unionized bargaining unit had to join *the union or pay equivalent fees to finance its collective bargaining services. Weak unions and racial divide and rule undermined King's hopes for a more prosperous and harmonious Southland.*

Unknown to King, the Georgia Commission on Education had sent an agent named Ed Friend to infiltrate and photograph the Highlander meeting. A month later, the commission sent a pamphlet to the Georgia legislature and the U.S. Congress purporting to show "Martin Luther King at a Communist training school." It pictured King sitting between Communist Party member Abner Berry (also unknown to King) and King's ally from Montgomery, Aubrey Williams, a staunch anti-communist liberal. The John Birch Society, the White Citizens' Council, and others sent postcards and plastered the highways with billboards of this photo and its glaring headline. Thus began the falsehood that King, one of the most famous Baptist preachers of his time, was a secret communist. Only his achievements as a religious and human rights leader ultimately discredited this absurd misrepresentation.

—◇◇—

Highlander Folk School
MONTEAGLE, TENNESSEE, SEPTEMBER 2, 1957

Mr. Chairman, Mr. Horton, distinguished guests, ladies, and gentlemen, it is a great privilege and a distinct honor for me to have the opportunity of being a part of the twenty-fifth anniversary observance of the Highlander Folk School. I have long admired the noble purpose and creative work of this institution. For twenty-five years you have stood with dauntless courage and fearless determination. You have given the South some of its most responsible leaders in this great period of transition. And so I am happy to congratulate you today for all of your great work, and hope for you many more years of creative and meaningful work.

I cannot begin my talk this morning without pausing to bring you greetings from Montgomery, Alabama. And I bring you special greetings from the fifty thousand Negro citizens of Montgomery who more than a year ago came to see that it is ultimately more honorable to walk in dignity than ride in humiliation. I bring you greetings from a people who were willing to substitute tired feet for tired souls, and walk the streets of Montgomery until the long night of enforced segregation in bus transportation had been removed.

I'm certainly happy to be here and to see in this audience Mrs. Rosa Parks. There couldn't, as we've just heard, you would not have had a Montgomery story without Rosa Parks. I'm also very happy to see in the audience my very close and competent associate, Ralph Abernathy. He has worked with me and the Montgomery community all of these months. And I'm sure that I voice the sentiment of Mrs. Parks and Reverend Abernathy and all of the fifty thousand Negro citizens of Montgomery when I say to you that we are eternally grateful to each of you for your moral support in our struggle for human dignity and first-class citizenship. Many of you sent financial contributions. Many of you were with us in spirit, and we realize that as we walked the streets of Montgomery, we did not walk alone, but hundreds and thousands of people of goodwill walked with us. And we are grateful to you for that. I'm also happy to share the speaking responsibilities this morning with Aubrey Williams, one of the noble personalities of our times. And I'm sure we will be eternally grateful to him for the work that he has done in the area of human relations and for the many things that he has done to make the South a better South and the world a better world.

I have been asked to speak from the subject: "A Look to the Future." In order to look to the future, it is often necessary to get a clear picture of the past. In order to know where we are going, it is often necessary to see from whence we have come. And so I begin with a survey of past developments in the area of race relations.

As we look over the long sweep of race relations in America we notice that there has been something of an evolutionary growth over the years. There have been at least three distinct periods in the history of race relations in this nation, each representing growth over a former period. It is interesting to note that in each period there finally came a decision from the Supreme Court to give legal and constitutional validity to the dominant thought patterns of that particular period. The first period in the area of race relations extended from 1619 to 1863. This was the period of slavery. During this period the Negro was an "it" rather than a "he," a thing to be used rather than a person to be respected. He was merely a depersonalized cog in a vast plantation machine. In 1857, toward the end of this period, there finally came a decision from the Supreme Court to give legal and constitutional validity to the whole system of slavery. This decision, known as the *Dred Scott* decision, stated in substance that the Negro is not a citizen of this nation; he is merely property subject to the dictates of his owner.

The second period in the development of race relations in America extended, broadly speaking, from 1863 to 1954. We may refer to this as the period of segregation. In 1896, through the famous *Plessy v. Ferguson* decision, the Supreme Court established the doctrine of separate but equal as the law of the land. Through this decision the dominant thought patterns of this second stage of race relations were given legal and constitutional validity. Now we must admit that this second period was something of an improvement over the first period of race relations because it at least freed the Negro from the bondage of physical slavery. But it was not the best stage because segregation is at bottom nothing but slavery covered up with certain niceties of complexity. So the end result of this second period was that the Negro ended up being plunged across the abyss of exploitation where he experienced the bleakness of nagging injustice.

The third period in the development of race relations in America had its beginning on May 17, 1954. You may refer to this as the period of complete and constructive integration. The Supreme Court's decision [*Brown v. Board of Education*], which came to give legal and constitutional validity to the dominant thought patterns of this period, said in substance that the old Plessy doctrine must go, that separate facilities were inherently unequal, that to segregate a child on the basis of his race is to deny that child of equal protection of the law. And so as a result of this decision we find ourselves standing on the threshold of the third and most constructive period in the development of race relations in the history of our nation. To put it in biblical terms, we have broken loose from the Egypt of slavery. We have moved through the wilderness of "separate but equal," and now we stand on the border of the promised land of integration.

The great moral challenge that confronts each of us at this moment is to work passionately and unrelentingly for the complete realization of the ideals and principles in this third period. We must not rest until segregation and discrimination have been liquidated from every area of our nation's life. As we stand at the threshold of this third period of race relations, we notice two contradictory forces at work in the South: the forces of defiance and the forces of compliance. On the one hand, we notice a resurgence of the Ku Klux Klan and the rise of White Citizens'

Councils. On the other hand, we notice constructive forces at work seeking to create a new respect for human dignity. In order to get a clear picture of the situation, we may look at each of these forces separately.

The past three years have witnessed the birth in the South of the U.S. Knights of the Ku Klux Klan. Almost dead for more than two decades, the Klan has staged a new revival. This organization is determined to preserve segregation at any cost; its methods are crude and criminative. Unlike the Klan of twenty years ago, this new Klan does not list among its members the so-called respectable people. It draws its members from the undereducated and underprivileged groups who see in the Negro's rising status a political and economic threat. And although the Klan will never regain the power that it once possessed, we must not take it lightly. Beneath the surface of all of its actions is the ugly theme of unleashed, unchallenged racial and religious bigotry. There is always the implied threat of violence.

Then there are the White Citizens' Councils. Since they operate on a higher political and economic level than the Klan, a halo of respectability hovers over them. But like the Klan, they are determined to preserve segregation and thereby defy the desegregation rulings of the Supreme Court. They base their defense on the legal maneuvers of interposition and nullification. Unfortunately for those who disagree with the councils, their methods do not stop with legal tactics; their methods range from threats and intimidation to economic reprisals against Negro men and women. These methods also extend to white persons who will dare to take a stand for justice. They demand absolute conformity from whites and abject submission from Negroes.

The effects of the councils' activities are not difficult to determine. First, they have brought many white moderates to the point that they no longer feel free to discuss the issues involved in desegregation for fear of what they will be labeled. The channels of communication between whites and Negroes are now closed. Certainly this is tragic. Men hate each other because they fear each other; they fear each other because they don't know each other; they don't know each other because they can't communicate with each other; they can't communicate with each other because they are separated from each other.

Another effect of the Citizens' Councils is that of opening the way for violence. It is true that they often piously argue that they abhor violence, but their defiance of the law, their unethical methods, and their vitriolic public denouncements actually create the atmosphere for violence. The White Citizens' Councils, along with the Ku Klux Klan, must be held responsible for all of the terror, mob rule, and brutal murders that have encompassed the South for the last several months.

There is another side to the South that counterbalances the Klan and the Councils. It is the work of hundreds of persons in the white South who realize that they cannot cut themselves off from the rest of the nation. They are working in numerous unpublicized ways to implement the rulings of the Supreme Court and make the ideal of brotherhood a reality. Desegregation, too, is appearing in hundreds of minute ways, and even in a few spectacular ways in all of the borderstates. It is visible on hundreds of college campuses in the South. It is gradually becoming visible in public schools of the South. Separate waiting rooms and restrooms are about gone from the airlines, trains, and buses. Negroes are gradually being elected to public offices in cities of the Deep South, and many ministerial associations are integrated. While the reactionary guardians of the status quo are busy crying "Never," the system of segregation is crumbling all around them.

Now, what of the future? First, let us admit that the reactionary forces of the white South present certain barriers to integration that will make the transition much more difficult. They will seek to delay integration as long as possible by a variety of legal tactics.

We must also face the fact that these delays are not merely the rearguard action of professional bigots. Many of the southerners who oppose integration believe with utter devoutness that what they do is best for themselves, their families, and their nation. This quality of sincerity makes the job of desegregation infinitely more difficult.

But in spite of all of this, the opponents of desegregation are fighting a losing battle. The Old South is gone, never to return again. Many of the problems that we are confronting in the South today grow out of the futile attempt of the white South to perpetuate a system of human values that came into being under a feudalistic plantation system which cannot survive in a day of democratic equalitarianism. Yes, the Old South is a lost cause.

We must gain consolation in the fact that there are constructive forces that will defeat in time all of the barriers of opposition.

First, if the South is to survive economically, it must inevitably industrialize. We see signs of this vigorous industrialization with the concomitant urbanization throughout every southern state. Day after day, the South is receiving new multimillion-dollar industries. With this growth of industry, the folkways of white supremacy will necessarily pass away. Moreover, southerners are learning to be good businessmen, and as such realize that bigotry is costly and bad for business. This growth of industry will increase the purchasing power of the Negro. And this augmented purchasing power will be reflected in more adequate housing, improved medical care, and greater educational opportunities. Each of these exemplifies further weakening of segregation.

It must also be stressed that as industry grows in the South, organized labor will become more influential in this section. Organized labor has proved to be one of the most powerful forces in removing the blight of segregation and discrimination from our nation. Labor leaders wisely realize that the forces that are anti-Negro are usually anti-labor, and vice versa. And so organized labor is one of the Negro's strongest allies in the struggle for freedom.

In spite of screams of "Over my dead body will any change come," one must not minimize the impact upon the South of federal court action. Federal court decrees have altered transportation patterns, educational mores, use of golf courses, and a myriad of other matters. These major social changes have a cumulative force condition-ing other segments of life. The South next reveals increas-ing sensitivity to the force of world opinion. Few indeed are the southerners who relish having their status lumped in the same category with the Union of South Africa as a final refuge of segregation. It is not pleasant either to be shown how southern intransigence fortifies Communist appeals to Asian and African peoples. Here is further crip-pling away at old patterns.

Also hopeful is the way in which human relation agen-cies of all types, public and private, are increasing their activities. Their still small voices go unheard many times amid the louder shouts of defiance, but their influence is felt and growing.

More and more, the voice of the Christian church is being heard. For many years we had to face the tragic fact that Sunday morning when we stood to sing, "In Christ There Is No East or West," was the most segregated hour in Christian America. Thank God we're beginning to shake the lethargy from our eyes and move in accord with the rhythmic beat of the music of justice. Churches all over the country are asking their members to reexamine their consciences, and to measure practice against profession. More and more the churches are willing to cry in terms of deep and patient faith: "Out of one blood, God has made all nations and men to dwell upon the face of the earth."

Lastly, the determination of the Negro himself to gain freedom and equality is the most powerful force that will ultimately defeat the barriers of integration. For many years the Negro passively accepted segregation. He was the victim of stagnant passivity and deadening complacency. The forces of slavery and segregation caused many Negroes to feel that perhaps they were inferior. But through the forces of history, something happened to the Negro. He came to feel that he was somebody. He came to feel that the important thing about a man is not his specificity but his fundamentum, not the color of his skin or the texture of his hair, but the texture and quality of his soul. With this new sense of dignity and new self-respect, a new Negro emerged. So there has been a revolutionary change in the Negro's evaluation of his nature and destiny, and a concomitant determination to achieve freedom and human dignity whatever the cost may be.

Fortunately, the Negro has been willing to grapple with a new and powerful approach to his problem in the South, namely nonviolence. It is my great hope that as the Negro plunges deeper into the quest for freedom, he will plunge deeper into the philosophy of nonviolence. As a race we must struggle passionately and unrelentingly to the goal of justice, but we must be sure that our hands are clean in the struggle. We must never struggle with falsehood, hate, or malice; we must never become bitter. We must never succumb to the temptation of using violence in the struggle, for if this happens, unborn generations will be the recipients of a long and desolate night of bitterness, and our chief legacy to the future will be an endless reign of meaningless chaos.

I realize that this approach will mean suffering and sacrifice. Some will ask, "What if these acts of violence continue and increase as a result of the Negro following this method? What then can be his defense?" His defense is to meet every act of violence toward an individual Negro with the fact that there are thousands of others who will present themselves in his place as potential victims. If the oppressors bomb the home of one Negro for his courage, then this must be met by the fact that they will be required to bomb the homes of hundreds and thousands of Negroes. If they deny bread and milk to Negro children whose parents want them to be free, then they must be required to deny these children every necessity of life: water and air itself. This dynamic unity, this amazing self-respect, this willingness to suffer and this refusal to hit back will soon cause the oppressor to become ashamed of his own methods. You will leave him glutted with his own barbarity; you will force him to stand before the world and his God splattered with the blood and reeking with the stench of his Negro brother. This, it seems to me, is the only valid answer.

With all of these forces working together, I am convinced that we can bring the third period of race relations in America to its full realization in the not too distant future. So my answer to the question of our theme is that the future is filled with vast and marvelous possibilities. This is a great time to be alive. Let us not despair. Let us realize that as we struggle for justice and freedom we have cosmic companionship. The arc of the moral universe is long, but it bends toward justice. As Carlyle says, "No lie can live forever." As William Cullen Bryant says, "Truth crushed to earth will rise again." As James Russell Lowell says,

Truth forever on the scaffold,
Wrong forever on the throne.
Yet that scaffold sways the future,
And behind the dim unknown
Stands God, within the shadow,
Keeping watch above His own.

And so let us go out and work with renewed vigor to make the unfolding work of destiny a reality in our generation. We must not slow up. Let us keep moving.

There are certain technical words in the vocabulary of every academic discipline which tend to become clichés and stereotypes. Psychologists have a word which is probably used more frequently than any other word in modern psychology. It is the word "maladjusted." This word is the ringing cry of the new child psychology. Now in a sense all of us must live the well-adjusted life in order to avoid neurotic and schizophrenic personalities. But there are some things in our social system to which I am proud to be maladjusted and to which I suggest that you, too, ought to be maladjusted. I never intend to adjust myself to the viciousness of mob rule. I never intend to adjust myself to the evils of segregation and the crippling effects of discrimination. I never intend to adjust myself to the tragic inequalities of an economic system which takes necessities from the masses to give luxuries to the classes. I never intend to become adjusted to the madness of militarism and the self-defeating method of physical violence. I call upon you to be maladjusted.

Well you see, it may be that the salvation of the world lies in the hands of the maladjusted. The challenge to you this morning as I leave you is to be maladjusted—as maladjusted as the prophet Amos, who in the midst of the injustices of his day, could cry out in terms that echo across the centuries, "Let judgment run down like waters and righteousness like a mighty stream"; as maladjusted as Lincoln, who had the vision to see that this nation could not survive half slave and half free; as maladjusted as Jefferson, who in the midst of an age amazingly adjusted to slavery could cry out in words lifted to cosmic proportions, "All men are created equal, and are endowed by their creator with certain inalienable rights, that among these are life, liberty, and the pursuit of happiness."

Yes, as maladjusted as Jesus of Nazareth who dared to dream a dream of the fatherhood of God and the brotherhood of man. He looked at men amid the intricate and fascinating military machinery of the Roman Empire, and could say to them, "He who lives by the sword will perish by the sword." Jesus, who could look at men in the midst of their tendencies for tragic hate and say to them, "Love your enemies. Bless them that curse you. Pray for them that despitefully use you." The world is in desperate need of such maladjustment. Through such maladjustment we will be able to emerge from the bleak and desolate midnight of man's inhumanity to man into the bright and glittering daybreak of freedom and justice.

II

*"It is a dark day indeed when
men cannot work to implement
the ideal of brotherhood without
being labeled communist."*

Ralph Helstein, president of the United Packinghouse Workers Union of America (UPWA), attended King's talk at Highlander, whose founder Myles Horton at that time served as the UPWA's educational director. Both of these white men had long fought for racial equality. Helstein publicly denounced Georgia governor Marvin Griffin for claiming that King and the southern civil rights movement were dupes of Communists. Within a month of the Highlander gathering, King spoke at the UPWA national contract and anti-discrimination conference in Chicago on October 2, 1957, a meeting that brought together racial minorities, women, and union advocates of equal rights. King gave virtually the same speech as at Highlander but prefaced it by expressing deep appreciation for the packinghouse union. He emphasized that "the forces that are anti-Negro are by and large anti-labor, and with the coming together of the powerful influence of labor and all people of goodwill in the struggle for freedom and human dignity, I can assure you that we have a powerful instrument." Following King's speech to the UPWA, African American rank-and-file activists, particularly women, expanded their various civil rights activities, and *the union sponsored a Fund for Democracy to support the southern civil rights movement, to which individual union members donated $11,000.*

The UPWA had the most advanced civil rights union program of its time and for good reason. The owners of the meat-packing industry had early on foiled unionization by playing European ethnic groups off one another; they then divided blacks and whites against each other during the horrific 1919 Chicago race riot that destroyed packinghouse organizing for a generation. In the 1930s, Communists and black activists made equality and interracial organizing founding principles as important to union success as the idea of plant-wide industrial organization. The UPWA became a prominent left-led union after World War II with a strong core of black and women leaders.

The UPWA escaped the CIO purge of eleven leftist unions that began in 1949, but barely. To appease the Taft-Hartley Act, the union demoted some of its Communist leaders and turned Helstein, nominally a non-Communist general counsel for the union, into its president. He protected the union by solidifying its black leadership, launching far-reaching desegregation campaigns, and filing grievances against racial discrimination. Helstein equated southern segregation with colonialism abroad and refused to support U.S. military interventions, and he and the union opposed the Korean War. The House Committee on Un-American Activities (HUAC) and the Senate Internal Security Subcommittee (SISS), led by Mississippi senator Eastland, held continuing hearings on the connection between "Communism" and civil rights in unions, including the UPWA.

In 1955, the AFL and CIO unions merged, and the labor movement became more conservative. The AFL-CIO adopted an ethics code that excluded Communists from leadership positions in its member unions and set up a committee to make sure its member unions complied with it. It was a time when segregationists physically attacked students who tried to integrate schools in Little Rock, Arkansas, and Prince Edward County, Virginia, where officials closed the public schools rather than desegregate them. In a time of anti-communist hysteria and "massive resistance" to integration, King served on a committee to monitor UPWA compliance with AFL-CIO anti-communist ethics and King helped to engineer a statement rejecting HUAC allegations against the union. With King's support, the UPWA weathered the Red Scare and remained within the AFL-CIO. It continued a remarkable civil rights campaign as one of King's most reliable and ardent advocates.

—◇◇◇—

United Packinghouse Workers Union of America
ATLANTA, GEORGIA, JUNE 11, 1959

After discovering that the House Committee on Un-American Activities had conducted hearings in the matter of the alleged Un-American activities in the United Packinghouse Workers of America, the executive committee of the Southern Christian Leadership Conference voted unanimously to publicly express its confidence in the integrity of this union.

The officers and members of the United Packinghouse Workers Union have demonstrated a real humanitarian concern. They have worked indefatigably to implement the ideals and principles of our democracy. Their devotion to the cause of civil rights has been unwavering. This union has stood out against segregation and discrimination not only in public pronouncements, but also in actual day to day practice. They have given thousands of dollars to aid organizations that are working for freedom and human dignity of the South. Because of the forthright stand of the packinghouse workers in the area of civil rights, they have aroused the ire of some persons who are not so committed. But in spite of this, they have continued to work courageously for the ideal of brotherhood of man. It is tragic indeed that some of our reactionary brothers in America will go to the limit of giving Communism credit for all good things that happen in our nation. It is a dark day indeed when men cannot work to implement the ideal of brotherhood without being labeled communist.

We sincerely hope that nothing will happen to deter the significant work being done by this dedicated labor organization. Again we express our confidence in the integrity and loyalty of the officers and members of the United Packinghouse Workers of America.

III

"We, the Negro people and labor . . . inevitably will sow the seeds of liberalism."

The United Automobile Workers (UAW) union and its charismatic president, Walter Reuther, provided powerful financial and organizational support for King and the southern civil rights movement, starting with $5,000 in donations to the Montgomery Bus Boycott. King came to see Reuther as one of his strongest allies. Reuther had led the purges against alleged Communists in the labor movement and had an ambivalent record on internal civil rights policies. African Americans held few significant offices and remained mostly blocked from workplace advancement in the auto industry, especially in the South, where Reuther moved cautiously against white privilege. As late as 1963, the UAW still had segregated locals in the South, and blacks made up only 1.5 percent of the union's skilled workers. The UAW did not elect an African American to its large executive board until 1962.

Despite difficulties integrating his own union, Reuther welcomed the direct action phase of the civil rights movement. He believed the black student sit-ins and freedom rides of 1960 and 1961 disrupted the "consensus" of the conformist Cold War era and provided an opening for *change. An ambitious organizer and expansive thinker with a huge union budget, Reuther and his 1.6 million–member union underwrote the "heyday of American liberalism" and became a major player with President Kennedy and his successor Lyndon B. Johnson. Many saw the UAW bureaucracy as stifling to rank-and-file democracy, yet few could deny that Reuther knew how to use his bureaucracy and budget to bring change at the legislative level.*

King's speech before the UAW at its twenty-fifth anniversary convention in 1961 thus strengthened a powerful alliance between the two leaders. King delivered this speech to 5,700 union members and guests—the overwhelming majority of them white men—in Detroit's Cobo Hall. King drew parallels between the auto sitdown strikes of 1936 that led to the UAW's success in bargaining with General Motors and the black student lunch counter sit-ins; he warned against automation that would sweep away unionized industrial jobs; he harked back to the enslavement and Jim Crow laws that had turned black workers into cheap labor; and he called for a powerful alliance between unions and the civil rights movement. The UAW newspaper Solidarity *also noted King's peace theme, headlining an article about the speech as "Nonviolence or Nonexistence." As at Highlander, King insisted that progress came only through hard work.*

In the aftermath of the speech, the UAW took up King's call for President Kennedy to issue a second Emancipation Proclamation for economic and civil rights reforms. Reuther, head of the AFL-CIO's Industrial Union Department and an architect of the merger between the CIO and the AFL, also called upon the federation to "put its own house in order" by making its members' unions comply with the federation's nondiscrimination policy.

—◇◇◇—

United Automobile Workers Union
DETROIT, MICHIGAN, APRIL 27, 1961

Mr. Chairman, President Reuther, distinguished secretary of labor Mr. [Arthur] Goldberg, Senator [Phillip] Hart, all of the distinguished guests assembled here on the platform, delegates and friends of UAW, ladies and gentlemen. I need not pause to say how very delighted I am to be here this evening and to be a part of this auspicious occasion, and I cannot stand here without giving just a word of thanks to this great union for all that you have done across these twenty-five years. You have made life more meaningful for millions of people, and I'm sure that America is a better place in which to live as a result of the great work that has been done by UAW. You have given to this nation a magnificent example of honest democratic trade unionism. And your great president, Walter Reuther, will certainly go down in history as one of the truly great persons of this generation. (Applause)

I bring greetings to you this evening from the hundreds and thousands—yea, millions of people in the Southland who are struggling for freedom and human dignity. I bring greetings to you from the thousands of Negro students who have stood up courageously against the principalities of segregation for all of these months they have moved in a uniquely meaningful orbit, imparting light and heat to distant satellites. And, as a result of their nonviolent and yet courageous struggle, they have been able to bring about integration in more than 139 cities at the lunch counters. (Applause) I am sure that when historians look back over this particular era of our history, they will have to record this movement as one of the most significant epics of our heritage.

Now, as I think with you tonight and think about this significant occasion, I would like to open by saying that organized labor has come a long, long way from the days of the strike-breaking injunctions of federal courts, from the days of intimidation and firings in the plants, from the days that your union leaders could be physically beaten with impunity. The clubs and claws of the heartless anti-labor forces have been clipped, and you now have organizations of strength and intelligence to keep your interest from being submerged and ignored. This is certainly the glorious meaning of your twenty-fifth anniversary.

Negroes who are now but beginning their march from the dark and desolate Egypt of segregation and discrimination can gain from you real inspiration and encouragement for the hard road still ahead. But though we have a multitude of problems almost absorbing every moment of our time and consuming almost every ounce of our energies, we cannot be unmindful of new problems confronting labor. And toward these problems we are not neutral because they are our problems as well.

The autoworkers are facing hard-core unemployment. New economic patterning through automation and relocation of plants is dissolving the nation's basic industries. This is to me a catastrophe. We are neither technologically advanced nor socially enlightened as a nation if we witness this disaster for tens of thousands without finding a solution. And by a solution I mean a real and genuine alternative providing the same living standards and opportunities which were swept away by a force called progress, but which for many is destruction.

A society that performs miracles with machinery has the capacity to make some miracles for men if it values men as highly as it values machines. This is really the crux of the problem. Are we as concerned for human values and human resources as we are for material and mechanical values? The automobile industry is not alone a production complex of assembly lines and steel-forming equipment. It is an industry of people who must live in decency with the security for children, for old age, for health and cultural life. Automation cannot be permitted to become a blind monster which grinds out more cars and simultaneously snuffs out the hopes and lives of the people by whom the industry was built.

Perhaps few people can so well understand the problems of autoworkers and others in labor as Negroes themselves, because we built a cotton economy for three hundred years as slaves on which the nation grew powerful, and we still lack the most elementary rights of citizens or workers. We, too, realize that when human values are subordinated to blind economic forces, human beings can become human scrap.

Our kinship was not born, however, with the rise of automation. In the birth of your organization as you confronted recalcitrant antagonists, you forged new weapons appropriate to your fight. Thus in the thirties, when industrial unionism sought recognition as a form of industrial democracy, there were powerful forces which said to you the same words we as Negroes hear now: "Never . . . You are not ready. . . . You are really seeking to change our form of society. . . . You are Reds. . . . You are troublemakers. . . . You are stirring up discontent and discord where none exists. . . . You are interfering with our property rights. . . . You are captives of sinister elements who would exploit you."

Both of us have heard these reckless charges. Both of us know that what we have sought were simple basic needs without which no man is a whole person. In your pursuit of these goals during the middle thirties, in part of your industry you creatively stood up for your rights by sitting down at your machines, just as our courageous students are sitting down at lunch counters across the South. They screamed at you and said that you were destroying property rights—but nearly thirty years later the ownership of the automobile industry is still in the hands of its stockholders and the value of its shares has multiplied manifold, producing profits of awesome size, and we are proudly borrowing your techniques, and though the same old and tired threats and charges have been dusted off for us, we doubt that we shall collectivize a single lunch counter or nationalize the consumption of sandwiches and coffee. (Applause)

Because you persisted in your quest for a better life, you brought new horizons to the whole nation. Industry after industry was compelled to civilize its practices and in so doing benefited themselves along with you. The new unions became social institutions, which stabilized the nation, fortified it, and thrust it up to undreamed of levels of production. There are more ties of kinship between labor and the Negro people than tradition. For example, labor needs a wage-hour bill which puts a firm floor under wage scales. Negroes need the same measures, even more desperately, for so many of us earn less than one dollar and twenty-five cents an hour. Labor needs housing legislation to protect it as a consumer. Negroes need housing legislation also. Labor needs an adequate old-age medical care bill and so do Negroes. The list might be extended ad infinitum for it is axiomatic that what labor needs, Negroes need, and simple logic therefore puts us side by side in the struggle for all elements in the decent standard of living.

As we survey the problems of labor from the chilling threat of automation to the needs in housing and social welfare generally, we confront the necessity to have a Congress responsive to liberal legislation. Here again the kinship of interests of labor and the Negro people expresses itself. Negroes need liberal congressmen if they are to realize equality and opportunity. The campaign to grant the ballot to Negroes in the South has profound implications. From all I have outlined, it is clear that the Negro vote would not be utilized in a vacuum. Negroes exercising a free suffrage would march to the polls to support those candidates who would be partial to social legislation. Negroes in the South, whether they elected white or Negro congressmen, would be placing in office a liberal candidate, if you will—a labor candidate. (Applause) No other political leader could have a program possessing appeal to Negroes.

In these circumstances, the campaign for Negro suffrage is both a fulfillment of constitutional rights and a fulfillment of labor's needs in a fast-changing economy. Therefore, I feel justified in asking you for your continued support in the struggle to achieve the ballot all over the nation and in the South in particular. We, the Negro people and labor, by extending the frontiers of democracy to the South, will inevitably sow the seed of liberalism, where reaction has flourished unchallenged for decades. A new day will dawn which will see militant, steadfast and reliable congressmen from the South joining those from the northern industrial states to design and enact legislation for the people rather than for the privileged.

Now, I need not say to you that this problem and all of the problems which we face in the nation and in the world, for that matter, will not work itself out. We know that if the problem is to be solved, we must work to solve it. Evolution may be true in the biological realm, but when we work to apply it to the whole of society, there is very little evidence for it. Social progress never rolls in on the wheels of inevitability. It comes through the tireless efforts and the persistent work of dedicated individuals. Without this hard work, time itself becomes the ally of the insurgent and primitive forces of social stagnation. So in order to realize the American dream of economic justice and of the brotherhood of man, men and women all over the nation must continue to work for it. . . .

We will continue to work, and work with the faith that this dream can be realized. I believe it will be realized. For although the arc of the moral universe is long it bends toward justice. Before this dream is realized, maybe some will have to get scarred up; before the dream is realized, maybe some will have to go to jail; before the dream is realized, maybe some will have to face physical death; but if physical death is the price that some must pay to free their children from a permanent life of psychological death, then nothing could be more honorable. (Applause)

There is something in this universe. So we must continue to struggle for economic justice—the brotherhood of man—with the conviction that there is something in this universe which justifies Carlyle in saying, "No lie can live forever." There is something in this universe which justifies William Cullen Bryant in saying, "Truth crushed to earth shall rise again." There is something in this universe which justifies James Russell Lowell in saying, "Truth forever on the scaffold, wrong forever on the throne. Yet that scaffold sways the future."

This is our hope. This is the faith that will carry us on and if we will stand by this and continue to work for the ideal, we will be able to bring into being that new day. This will be the day when all of God's children, black men and white men, Jews and Gentiles, Protestants and Catholics, will be able to join hands and sing anew with the Negro slaves of old, "Free at last, free at last, thank God Almighty, we are free at last!" (Applause)

IV

If the Negro Wins, Labor Wins

George Meany—*a white plumber from New York who boasted that he had never been in a strike or even on a picket line—became AFL-CIO president with the 1955 merger and was in his mid-sixties by 1961. He and the federation had done little more for civil rights than pass nominal resolutions and listen to reports from its Civil Rights Committee (chaired by white males). Dissatisfied with the AFL-CIO performance, the National Association for the Advancement of Colored People (NAACP), under the leadership of its labor secretary, Herbert Hill, undertook a series of investigations of racism that tainted many unions. At the AFL-CIO's 1959 convention, A. Philip Randolph, one of the federation's two black vice presidents, spoke out against railroad brotherhoods that prohibited blacks from membership in their constitutions and building trades unions that excluded or segregated black workers. In the same year, Randolph and other black trade unionists also organized the Negro American Labor Council (NALC) to pressure the federation and its member unions. In February 1961, the NALC held a meeting of five hundred members that heard speeches by King, UPWA president Ralph Helstein, and others demanding*

equal rights and condemning racism among various
unions within the AFL-CIO.

In a war of words, Randolph accused the AFL-CIO
of "moral paralysis, pessimism, defeatism, and cynicism."
He said the federation should exercise the same vigor in
disciplining or expelling racist unions as it had in expel-
ling unions supposedly dominated by Communists. (The
American Federation of Teachers earlier did expel its seg-
regated southern locals.) At the AFL-CIO's 1959 conven-
tion, Meany had testily asked Randolph, "Who in the hell
appointed you as guardian of the Negro [union] members
in America?" The AFL-CIO executive committee later
set up a three-person subcommittee that wrote a report
censuring Randolph and blaming him for widening the
gap between the black community and the unions. Black
newspapers played up the conflict and the New York
Times *editorialized that the AFL-CIO was "knocking at*
the wrong door" in blaming Randolph for trouble in la-
bor's race relations. King called the censure of Randolph
"shocking and deplorable." Herbert Hill, at the NAACP
annual meeting in January 1961, published a scorching
report on union racism in the five years since the merger
of the AFL-CIO.

King stepped into this loaded, tense atmosphere at
the AFL-CIO's Fourth Constitutional Convention at the
Americana Hotel in Bal Harbour, a suburb of Miami
Beach, in December 1961. On day one, President Meany
began his fourth two-year term to a standing ovation of
three thousand delegates and started the convention with
a vitriolic speech condemning Communism and putting
unions on the side of U.S. foreign policy. President John F.
Kennedy immediately followed, praising unions as a bul-
wark of American freedom. On day three, King spoke to
an audience consisting mostly of older white male union
leaders who gained their ascendency in the 1930s but

who now discussed union issues near the seashore in upscale hotels.

His AFL-CIO speech remains perhaps King's most well-known call for a special and enduring alliance between African Americans and organized labor. King came to the AFL-CIO convention in Miami Beach after a lengthy flight from Los Angeles and through Chicago after bad weather canceled his first flight. Undoubtedly fatigued, King addressed the unionists in sober fashion, obviously reading a speech that provided few openings for applause (and, indeed, there was little of it). He began by painting a picture of the exploitation of workers in pre-union days and made a classic appeal for unity of unions and civil rights forces that could improve the lot of all workers but especially those at the bottom. But King did not allow members of his audience to clap themselves on the back for a job well done. Randolph had mentored King and repeatedly organized defense funds when southern authorities tried to imprison him on phony charges, and King vigorously backed up Randolph in his conflicts with the AFL-CIO.

In a balanced but critical tone, King urged "thoughtful examination of Randolph's criticism of labor's efforts to end discrimination within its own ranks" and spelled out some of the ways the unions had disappointed civil rights proponents. King's complaints included a previous plan by AFL-CIO unions to raise two million dollars for the civil rights movement that never materialized. The relatively tiny UPWA had done much more than the awesome AFL-CIO to help finance the southern movement. The black newspaper the Chicago Defender *called King's speech a "sound rap on the knuckles of the world's largest and most powerful labor federation."*

But King's speech also outlined the basis for what Randolph called the "Negro-labor alliance" and affirmed the idea that "if the Negro wins, labor wins." King cited black voters helping to defeat a ban on the union shop in Louisiana as one example of how the civil rights movement could help labor. But King also sounded a dire warning against deindustrialization, racial division, and the rise of an ultra-right alliance between business, Republicans, and southern Democrats. Unless stopped by a powerful labor–civil rights and community alliance, he argued, the ultra-right would threaten "everything decent and fair in American life." In a chilling prediction of organized labor's future decline, he said failure to meet this challenge potentially could "drive labor into impotency." King thus offered a prophetic challenge to unions that seemed to be at the height of their power but, in fact, remained highly vulnerable. King pointed out as well that the ultra-right, not "scattered reds," posed the real threat to unions.

In this speech, King helped Randolph break the silence around the AFL-CIO's internal racism. The next day delegates followed King's speech with discussions of reports and resolutions on civil rights, led off by Randolph. The UPWA's Charles Hayes praised King's speech and called on the AFL-CIO "to close the gap" between fine resolutions and real action, while the UPWA's Russell Lasley also pointed out that there were "only a handful of Negro delegates present here." The AFL-CIO convention responded by passing a major civil rights program but did not raise the funds for civil rights King had hoped for. Meany had praised King and pinned a union button on his jacket to great applause, but the federation never brought King back to another national convention. The federation also failed to endorse the most famous mass march in American history, the 1963 March on Washington. Yet King's speech and the escalation of the civil rights movement did make a major impact on organized labor. Pushed also by the UAW, the AFL-CIO subsequently pro-

vided much of the pressure to pass the Civil Rights and Voting Rights acts of 1964 and 1965, and Meany spoke repeatedly in favor of desegregation and equal rights.

Four days after King's AFL-CIO speech, FBI director J. Edgar Hoover discovered that King's trusted New York advisor and fund-raiser Stanley Levison had written its first draft. Levison once raised funds for the Communist Party (CP) and although Hoover knew that he had completely broken his ties with the party in 1957, Hoover led President Kennedy to believe that Levison remained a CP member. The FBI also warned Kennedy about Hunter Pitts (Jack) O'Dell, who had been purged from the National Maritime Union during the Red Scare. After being purged, O'Dell defiantly joined but later quit the CP to work full-time with King in voter registration and fund-raising. President Kennedy insisted that King fire O'Dell, and he did. In response to the unfounded fears stirred up by Hoover, Attorney General Robert F. Kennedy also ordered FBI wiretapping and surveillance of King's associates and recorded King's conversations as well. This violation of privacy and constitutional rights expanded and continued under two presidents until King's death. It began with the FBI's obsession with King's allies in the labor left.

—◆◇◆—

AFL-CIO Fourth Constitutional Convention
MIAMI BEACH, FLORIDA, DECEMBER 11, 1961

President Meany, delegates to the Fourth Constitutional Convention of AFL-CIO, ladies and gentlemen . . .

Less than a century ago the laborer had no rights, little or no respect, and led a life which was socially submerged and barren.

He was hired and fired by economic despots whose power over him decreed his life or death. The children of workers had no childhood and no future. They, too, worked for pennies an hour, and by the time they reached their teens they were worn-out old men, devoid of spirit, devoid of hope and devoid of self-respect. Jack London described a child worker in these words: "He did not walk like a man. He did not look like a man. He was a travesty of the human. It was a twisted and stunted and nameless piece of life that shambled like a sickly ape, arms loose-hanging, stoop-shouldered, narrow-chested, grotesque and terrible." American industry organized misery into sweatshops and proclaimed the right of capital to act without restraints and without conscience.

Victor Hugo, literary genius of that day, commented bitterly that there was always more misery in the lower classes than there was humanity in the upper classes. The inspiring answer to this intolerable and dehumanizing existence was economic organization through trade unions. The worker became determined not to wait for charitable impulses to grow in his employer. He constructed the means by which a fairer sharing of the fruits of his toil had to be given to him or the wheels of industry, which he alone turned, would halt and wealth for no one would be available.

This revolution within industry was fought bitterly by those who blindly believed their right to uncontrolled profits was a law of the universe, and that without the maintenance of the old order, catastrophe faced the nation.

But history is a great teacher. Now everyone knows that the labor movement did not diminish the strength of the nation but enlarged it. By raising the living standards of millions, labor miraculously created a market for industry and lifted the whole nation to undreamed of levels of production. Those who today attack labor forget these simple truths, but history remembers them.

Labor's next monumental struggle emerged in the thirties when it wrote into federal law the right freely to organize and bargain collectively. It was now apparently emancipated. The days when workers were jailed for organizing, and when in the English Parliament Lord Macauley had to debate against a bill decreeing the death penalty for anyone engaging in a strike, were grim but almost forgotten memories. Yet, the Wagner Act, like any other legislation, tended merely to declare rights but did not deliver them. Labor had to bring the law to life by exercising in practice its rights over stubborn, tenacious opposition. It was warned to go slow, to be moderate, not to stir up trouble. But labor knew it was always the right time to do right, and it spread its organization over the nation and achieved equality organizationally with capital. The day of economic democracy was born.

Negroes in the United States read this history of labor and find that it mirrors their own experience. We are confronted by powerful forces telling us to rely on the goodwill and understanding of those who profit by exploiting us. They deplore our discontent, they resent our will to organize, so that we may guarantee that humanity will prevail and equality will be exacted. They are shocked that action organizations, sit-ins, civil disobedience, and protests are becoming our everyday tools, just as strikes, demonstrations, and union organization became yours to ensure that bargaining power genuinely existed on both sides of the table. We want to rely upon the goodwill of those who would oppose us. Indeed, we have brought forward the method of nonviolence to give an example of unilateral goodwill in an effort to evoke it in those who have not yet felt it in their hearts. But we know that if we are not simultaneously organizing our strength, we will have no means to move forward. If we do not advance, the crushing burden of centuries of neglect and economic deprivation will destroy our will, our spirits, and our hopes. In this way labor's historic tradition of moving forward to create vital people as consumers and citizens has become our own tradition, and for the same reasons.

This unity of purpose is not an historical coincidence. Negroes are almost entirely a working people. There are pitifully few Negro millionaires and few Negro employers. Our needs are identical with labor's needs: decent wages, fair working conditions, livable housing, old-age security, health and welfare measures, conditions in which families can grow, have education for their children, and respect in the community. That is why Negroes support labor's demands and fight laws which curb labor. That is why the labor-hater and labor-baiter is virtually always a twin-headed creature spewing anti-Negro epithets from one mouth and anti-labor propaganda from the other mouth. (Applause)

The duality of interests of labor and Negroes makes any crisis which lacerates you, a crisis from which we bleed. And as we stand on the threshold of the second half of the twentieth century, a crisis confronts us both. Those who in the second half of the nineteenth century could not tolerate organized labor have had a rebirth of power and seek to regain the despotism of that era while retaining the wealth and privileges of the twentieth century. Whether it be the ultra-right wing in the form of Birch societies or the alliance which former President Eisenhower denounced, the alliance between big military and big business, or the coalition of southern Dixiecrats and northern reactionaries, whatever the form, these menaces now threaten everything decent and fair in American life. Their target is labor, liberals, and Negro people, not scattered "reds" or

even Justice Warren, former presidents Eisenhower and
Truman and President Kennedy, who are in truth beyond
the reach of their crude and vicious falsehoods.

Labor today faces a grave crisis, perhaps the most ca-
lamitous since it began its march from the shadows of
want and insecurity. In the next ten to twenty years, automation will grind jobs into dust as it grinds out unbeliev-
able volumes of production. This period is made to order
for those who would seek to drive labor into impotency
by viciously attacking it at every point of weakness. Hard-
core unemployment is now an ugly and unavoidable fact of
life. Like malignant cancer, it has grown year by year and
continues its spread. But automation can be used to generate an abundance of wealth for people or an abundance of
poverty for millions as its humanlike machines turn out
human scrap along with machine scrap as a by-product of
production. And, I am convinced that our society, with its
ability to perform miracles with machinery, has the capacity to make some miracles for men—if it values men as
highly as it values machines. (Applause)

To find a great design to solve a grave problem, labor
will have to intervene in the political life of the nation
to chart a course which distributes the abundance to all
instead of concentrating it among a few. The strength to
carry through such a program requires that labor know its
friends and collaborate as a friend. If all that I have said is
sound, labor has no firmer friend than the twenty million
Negroes whose lives will be deeply affected by the new
patterns of production.

Now to say that we are friends would be an empty plat-
itude if we fail to behave as friends and honestly look to
weaknesses in our relationship. And unfortunately there
are weaknesses. Labor has not adequately used its great
power, its vision, and resources to advance Negro rights.
Undeniably, it has done more than other forces in Ameri-

can society to this end. Aid from real friends in labor has often come when the flames of struggle heighten. But Negroes are a solid component within the labor movement and a reliable bulwark for labor's whole program, and should expect more from it exactly as a member of a family expects more from his relatives than he expects from his neighbors.

Labor, which made impatience for long-delayed justice for itself a vital motive force, cannot lack understanding of the Negro's impatience. It cannot speak with the reactionaries' calm indifference, of progress around some obscure corner not yet possible even to see. There is a maxim in the law—justice too long delayed is justice denied. When a Negro leader who has a reputation of purity and honesty which has benefitted the whole labor movement criticizes it, his motives should not be reviled nor his earnestness rebuked. Instead, the possibility that he is revealing a weakness in the labor movement which it can ill afford should receive thoughtful examination. A man who has dedicated his long and faultless life to the labor movement cannot be raising questions harmful to it any more than a lifelong devoted parent can become the enemy of his child. The report of a committee may smother with legal constructions a list of complaints and dispose of it for the day. But if it buries a far larger truth, it has disposed of nothing and made justice more elusive.

Discrimination does exist in the labor movement. It is true that organized labor has taken significant steps to remove the yoke of discrimination from its own body. But in spite of this, some unions, governed by the racist ethos, have contributed to the degraded economic status of the Negro. Negroes have been barred from membership in certain unions and denied apprenticeship training and vocational education. In every section of the country, one can find labor unions existing as a serious and vicious obstacle when the Negro seeks jobs or upgrading in employment. Labor must honestly admit these shameful conditions, and design the battle plan which will defeat and eliminate them. In this way, labor would be unearthing the big truth and utilizing its strength against the bleakness of injustice in the spirit of its finest traditions. (Applause)

How can labor rise to the heights of its potential statesmanship and cement its bonds with Negroes to their mutual advantage?

First—labor should accept the logic of its special position with respect to Negroes and the struggle for equality. Although organized labor has taken actions to eliminate discrimination in its ranks, the standard expected of you is higher than the standard for the general community. Your conduct should and can set an example for others, as you have done in other crusades for social justice. You should root out vigorously every manifestation of discrimination so that some internationals, central labor bodies, or locals may not besmirch the positive accomplishments of labor. I am aware that this is not easy nor popular—but the eight-hour day was not popular nor easy to achieve. Nor was a closed shop, nor was a right to strike, nor was outlawing anti-labor injunctions. But you accomplished all of these with a massive will and determination. Out of such struggle for democratic rights, you won both economic gains and the respect of the country, and you will win both again if you will make Negro rights a great crusade.

Second—the political strength you are going to need to prevent automation from becoming a Moloch, consuming jobs and contract gains, can be multiplied if you tap the vast reservoir of Negro political power. Negroes given the vote will vote liberal and labor because they need the same liberal legislation labor needs.

To give just an example of the importance of the Negro vote to labor, I might cite the arresting fact that the only state in the South which repealed the right-to-work law is Louisiana. This was achieved because the Negro vote in that state grew large enough to become a balance of power, and it went along with labor to wipe out anti-labor legislation. (Applause) Thus, support to assist us in securing the vote can make the difference between success and defeat for us both. You have organizing experience we need, and you have an apparatus unparalleled in the nation. You recognized five years ago a moral opportunity and responsibility when several of your leaders, including Mr. Meany, Mr. Reuther, Mr. [David] Dubinsky [president of the International Ladies Garment Workers Union (ILGWU)], and Mr. [David] McDonald [president of the United Steelworkers of America (USWA)] and others, projected a $2 million campaign to assist the struggling Negroes fighting bitterly in handicapped circumstances in the South. A $10,000 contribution was voted by the ILGWU to begin the drive, but for reasons unknown to me, the drive was never begun.

The cost to us in lack of resources during these turbulent, violent years is hard to describe. We are mindful that many unions thought of as immorally rich, in truth, have problems in meeting the budget to properly service their members. So we do not ask that you tax your treasuries. Indeed, we ask that you appeal to your members for one dollar apiece to make democracy real for millions of deprived American citizens. For this you have the experience, the organization, and, most of all, the understanding.

If you would do these two things now in this convention—resolve to deal effectively with discrimination and provide financial aid for our struggle in the South—this convention will have a glorious moral deed to add to an illustrious history.

The two most dynamic and cohesive liberal forces in the country are the labor movement and the Negro freedom movement. Together we can be architects of democracy in a South now rapidly industrializing. Together we can retool the political structure of the South, sending to Congress steadfast liberals who, joining with those from northern industrial states, will extend the frontiers of democracy for the whole nation. Together we can bring about the day when there will be no separate identification of Negroes and labor. There is no intrinsic difference as I have tried to demonstrate. Differences have been contrived by outsiders who seek to impose disunity by dividing brothers because the color of their skin has a different shade. I look forward confidently to the day when all who work for a living will be one with no thought of their separateness as Negroes, Jews, Italians, or any other distinctions.

This will be the day when we shall bring into full realization the dream of American democracy—a dream yet unfulfilled. A dream of equality of opportunity, of privilege and property widely distributed; a dream of a land where men will not take necessities from the many to give luxuries to the few; a dream of a land where men will not argue that the color of a man's skin determines the content of his character; a dream of a nation where all our gifts and resources are held not for ourselves alone but as instruments of service for the rest of humanity; the dream of a country where every man will respect the dignity and worth of human personality—that is the dream.

As we struggle to make racial and economic justice a reality, let us maintain faith in the future. At times we confront difficult and frustrating moments in the struggle to make justice a reality, but we must believe somehow that these problems can be solved.

There is a little song that we sing in the movement taking place in the South. It goes something like this, "We shall overcome. We shall overcome. Deep in my heart I do believe, we shall overcome." And somehow all over America we must believe that we shall overcome and that these problems can be solved, and they will be solved. Before the victory is won, some of us will have to get scarred up, but we shall overcome. Before the victory of justice is a reality, some may even face physical death. But if physical death is the price that some must pay to free their children and their brothers from a permanent life of psychological death, then nothing could be more moral. Before the victory is won some more will have to go to jail. We must be willing to go to jail and transform the jails from dungeons of shame to havens of freedom and human dignity. (Applause) Yes, before the victory is won, some will be misunderstood. Some will be dismissed as dangerous rabble-rousers and agitators. Some will be called reds and Communists merely because they believe in economic justice and the brotherhood of man. But we shall overcome.

I am convinced that we shall overcome because the arc of the moral universe is long but it bends toward justice. We shall overcome because Carlyle is right, "No lie can live forever." We shall overcome because William Cullen Bryant is right, "Truth crushed to earth will rise again." We shall overcome because James Russell Lowell is right, "Truth forever on the scaffold, wrong forever on the throne. Yet that scaffold sways the future."

And so if we will go out with this faith and with this determination to solve these problems, we will bring into being that new day and that new America. When that day comes, the fears of insecurity and the doubts clouding our future will be transformed into radiant confidence, into glowing excitement to reach creative goals, and into an abiding moral balance where the brotherhood of man will be undergirded by a secure and expanding prosperity for all.

Yes, this will be the day when all of God's children, black men and white men, Jews and Gentiles, Protestants and Catholics, will be able to join hands all over this nation and sing in the words of the old Negro spiritual: "Free at last, free at last, thank God Almighty, we are free at last." (Applause)

V

*"I am in one of those houses
of labor to which I come not
to criticize, but to praise."*

U PWA president Ralph Helstein had been educating
his membership for years about corruption from
America's "commercial values," the dangers of racism
and militarism, and the need to mobilize workers and
communities for a holistic solution to the problems of
society. In turn, members of the union pushed Helstein
and the UPWA forward into a vigorous civil rights crusade. UPWA vice president Russell Lasley and other
black union activists worked with King from Montgomery forward and helped him organize a march for voting
rights on the nation's capitol in 1957. They also joined
defense committees for King when he came under attack,
and the UPWA donated 80 percent of the cost of SCLC's
budget in its first year. UPWA members gave individual
donations of financial support to student sit-ins, freedom
rides, and African Americans kicked out of their homes
in Fayette County, Tennessee, for trying to vote. The
UPWA continuously organized conferences and legislative actions to obtain equal rights for racial minorities
and women. Women came to the forefront in mobilizing
support for civil rights, and in August 1961, the union al-
located $14,000, raised from its individual members for

*its Fund for Democracy, to be used in the South. UPWA
members also fought for civil rights in their own communities (see the introduction).*

*This union's expansive views of the labor–civil rights
alliance contrasted to the staid bread-and-butter unionism and crusading anti-communism of the AFL-CIO.
When King came to Minneapolis, Minnesota, to speak at
the UPWA's national convention six months after speaking to the AFL-CIO in Miami Beach he expressed relief
to be in an interracial union with clear internal policies in
support of equality. After his speech the union donated
another $5,000 to King's movement, and its members
continued to organize interracial voter registration drives
throughout the Midwest and South and to challenge segregationist practices by some of its white members.*

*As President Helstein introduced King to the con-
vention at 2:00 p.m., convention delegates rose to give
King a great ovation. Perhaps as another effort to fend
off the continuing charges of Communism directed at
the UPWA by the House Un-American Activities Committee, according to the* Chicago Defender, *King declared
that Communism "has never attracted more than a tiny
group of Negroes"—a statement the paper played up with
a headline, "Neither Reds Nor Black Supremacy Appeal
to Negroes, King Declares." This statement does not appear quite that way in King's remarks transcribed in the
UPWA convention proceedings, or in King's written text,
which is the version of the speech we present here. In his
written speech, King's concern focused on the UPWA's
full-bore support of equal rights as compared to the con-
flicted posture of many other unions. King continued to
call for union support for the burgeoning freedom movement in the South.*

*In appealing to this extraordinary interracial union
that workers had forged, King called on "we who are the*

economically maimed and injured" to "stand together and act together" and paid tribute to "the ordinary people" in unions who "called their dream democracy." But he also warned of "impending economic hurricanes" caused by mechanization and the stranglehold of Democratic segregationists and Republican conservatives on the committees of the U.S. Congress. Tragically, of all the major unions of the 1960s, the UPWA got hit hardest by automation. Mechanization destroyed so many jobs in the packinghouse industry that in 1968 the union was forced to merge with the Amalgamated Meat Cutters and Butcher Workmen's union of the old AFL. This ended the distinctive civil rights unionism of the UPWA in the tradition of the old CIO.

—◇◇—

United Packinghouse Workers Union of America

MINNEAPOLIS, MINNESOTA, MAY 21, 1962

A few months ago, I addressed the AFL-CIO National Convention, and mindful that the unfulfilled needs of labor and the civil rights movement are serious, I appealed for the closest unity of our forces. To achieve that unity I felt we should be candid and frank with each other about weaknesses which diminish our effective cooperation. The two areas of criticism with which I dealt were labor's failure to use its strength internally to wipe out discrimination in unions, and the inadequate aid furnished to the civil rights struggles by labor.

It is not pleasant to criticize those who are friends, and the task was a difficult but necessary experience.

But this afternoon my mood is quite different. This afternoon I am in one of those houses of labor to which I come not to criticize, but to praise.

The United Packinghouse Workers of America has set an example for every democratic organization in the nation. Indeed, if labor as a whole, if the administration in Washington, matched your concern and your deeds, the civil rights problem would not be a burning national shame, but a problem long solved and in its solution a luminous accomplishment in the best tradition of American principles.

In the early days of organization of our Southern Christian Leadership Conference, you employed the shop collection to raise significant funds for us. As we continued our struggles for human dignity, you remained a constant supporter in some of our darkest hours when the most savage elements among our adversaries took control.

Your dependable help was like a mighty fortress protecting us. Your aid, however, went beyond money. When various city and state officials of the state of Alabama, in abuse of legitimate judicial process, instituted a series of libel suits against us in an attempt to wreck our leadership, you provided brilliant legal aid through your union council to strengthen our defense.

The debt we owe you is great, and we cannot repay you today, but our memory is long and our gratitude is lasting, and when the day comes when we have won victories enough to have some surplus strength, it will be yours to command.

Another proud distinction your union possesses is its record of dealing with discrimination internally. In the last analysis, this is an acid test. It is not easy and it is rarely accomplished completely because the whole of our society is pulsing with racism, but the steps you have taken are longer and more decisive than others can boast. Indeed, though I am no historian of labor, I feel safe in saying that even within the CIO tradition where discrimination was fought with conscious purpose your record is the best. In

America today this is the highest expression of patriotism and moral responsibility.

It is never easy to pioneer, but you did it while organizing a powerful industry whose abuses of public welfare were so extreme that they became a legend recorded in our literature by Upton Sinclair in his book *The Jungle*. That jungle was finally cleared and civilized by legislation and the adoption of socially responsible practices.

However, today a new jungle is creeping back, swallowing up and nullifying the achievements of the past, and this new jungle is not a wilderness of nature. It has the shining glittering face of science. It consists of the negative effects of automation and the runaway shop.

Both of these are destroying your jobs, changing your lives, while plans to counteract their destructive effects are either inadequate or nonexistent. . . .

We have become familiar with the fears that grip mankind as it sees the blinding terror of nuclear weapons. We know they must be controlled or we will live on the razor edge of annihilation. It has made us wonder if our technological genius has not outstripped our social and moral capabilities.

Though harnessing the awesome power of nuclear weapons is our greatest problem, we have another problem bequeathed to us by the accelerated progress of science. As machines replace men, we must again question whether the depth of our social thinking matches the growth of technological creativity. We cannot create machines which revolutionize industry unless we simultaneously create ideas commensurate with social and economic reorganization, which harness the power of such machines for the benefit of man. . . . The new age will not be an era of hope but of fear and emptiness unless we master this problem.

Its solution will require forthright creative social planning from the shop level up to the highest levels of government. It is here that the identity of interest of the labor movement and that of the civil rights movement merges. Negroes are already deeply affected by the unemployment engendered by automation. Long years of deprivation of opportunity have robbed us of the skills needed to utilize new industrial devices. Thus, even before we have achieved elementary human rights, many of us are threatened by catastrophic economic disabilities.

Like you, we are deeply concerned with minimum wages, with social security, with health measures. We, along with you, want housing fit for families to live in happily and comfortably. Like you, we want job certainty in our working days and retirement security when we grow old. A society as dynamic as ours can provide these things if it is as flexible and inventive as the science which is such a vital part of it. . . .

To take hold of these problems, we who are the economically maimed and injured must stand together and act together in order to compel government action swiftly and extensively. The federal government meets natural disasters promptly. It boldly organizes for national defense. It must deal with the impending economic hurricanes with similar decisiveness. For so many of us the same life or death questions are involved.

To influence our government in this constructive direction we shall need new and multiplied political strength. We have [many] Negroes [who] are excluded from social and political life. Millions have no vote locally and nationally. The crusade to put the ballot in the hands of people who share and understand your needs will benefit both you and them. It is well known that the forces which have historically blocked necessary social legislation are the political leaders from the South. I need only remind you that the chairmanship[s] of nine of the sixteen standing committees of the Senate is occupied by segregationists, while

the chairmanship of twelve of the twenty standing committees of the House are similarly occupied.

Thus, the politically Neanderthal views of southern
congressmen, protected by the shield of seniority, forged
out of years of disenfranchisement of the Negro voter,
dominate the key committees of Congress. They hold the
president's programs hostage, throttling our nation with
a nineteenth-century philosophy while the whirlwinds of
twentieth-century storms sweep away our security and
progress. When Negroes in the South receive the franchise,
they will use it not only for their own progress, but for all.
They, with labor, and other modern-thinking citizens will
support liberal-thinking candidates with programs ben-
efiting ordinary people, not merely the overprivileged. The
composition of Congress will thus undergo a face-lifting,
and social legislation will not be blocked by southern representatives, but will be written by them.

When the glorious sunlight of Negro freedom shines
throughout the land, the day of more freedom for all will
dawn. The struggle for civil rights is a fight for human
dignity in its broadest dimensions. In our complex society,
to fight against the inequities and injustices of segregation
and discrimination for the lowliest becomes a noble battle
in defense of the interests of everyone who works. Our victories will pay you dividends, and perhaps in this way we
will pay you the debt we owe for your magnificent support
over the years.

Years ago, it became a proud boast of the packing industry that by the application of science no part of the
animal was wasted. "Everything but the squeal of the pig"
was converted into a socially useful product. It is fair to
say that if this could be done by one industry with *pigs,* all
of society should seem capable of progress without wasting any *people!* This is the achievable task of the new age.

We will have no fear of the future if we master together

the task of the present. So much that we have already done together proves that in going further and strengthening our ties we will inevitably enrich the lives of all of us, bringing democratic dynamism into the political bloodstream of the nation. Lest we forget, the men who established our country were in the main ordinary people—but they had an extraordinary dream that all problems could be solved by united action; by participation of all upon an equal basis.

They called their dream democracy. Nearly two hundred years later, if we now faithfully develop and practice democracy, transforming it into living reality for all of our citizens, it will fashion a new era of abundance in material and moral riches.

[In King's remarks at the UPWA convention, King concluded with extemporaneous refrains he frequently used: the importance of being maladjusted, his faith in the future, a quote from James Russell Lowell about the arc of the moral universe bending toward justice, and he finished with "free at last, free at last, thank God Almighty, we are free at last."]

VI

"There are three major social evils ... the evil of war, the evil of economic injustice, and the evil of racial injustice."

When King came to speak at this gathering, District 65's convention, in 1962, he knew he was among friends. Secretary-Treasurer Cleveland Robinson said District 65 scarcely held a major event that King did not attend (he had spoken to the union in 1959 and several times in 1961), and the union and its members closely followed his 1962 civil rights campaign in Albany, Georgia. African Americans and Puerto Ricans working in the lowest stations in department stores and other phases of retail and wholesale work comprised 90 percent of the union's membership. Instead of his measured, sober, and formal manner so evident at some of his other union speeches, King preached to members of District 65, bringing the exuberance of southern church meetings to union members in the North. And while he had avoided this topic at the AFL-CIO, at District 65, King spoke freely about the devastating connections between racism, militarism, and war. He saw in its members and leaders the kind of movement that could reform society from the bottom up.

Like the packinghouse workers union, District 65 had long provided solid support to King. Robinson worked closely with A. Philip Randolph and was vice president of

*the Negro American Labor Council (NALC). More than
any other of King's labor advisors, he kept prodding King
to move toward union and economic justice issues within
King's SCLC. District 65 mounted picket lines and protests in New York in support of King's campaigns in the
South. The union affiliated to the Retail, Wholesale and
Department Store Union (RWDSU), a New York–based
grouping of unions that began under Communist leadership but later continued under a militant anti-communist
president; District 65 later joined the UAW. Whatever
their political stance, most union leaders prioritized a
pragmatic concern for union autonomy and the ability
to deliver for their membership, and District 65 was no
different.*

*King gave this speech on the opening day of the union's
convention outside New York City, fresh from a jail cell
in Albany, Georgia. For demanding the right to access
public facilities, decent schools, and to vote, King and
thousands of others had been herded into trucks and ar-
rested. Although producing no visible victories, the Albany movement unearthed a tremendous youthful spirit
of singing, marching, and praying. In a similar spirit,
King's audience at the District 65 convention cheered,
shouted, laughed, sang, and raised a fuss. After King's
death, the union made King's birthday a day off in its
contracts, and workers donated the proceeds of that day's
missed labor to a fund supporting human rights activity. The District 65 newspaper reproduced some of this
speech in its October 1962 edition, supplemented here
by excerpts from a recorded album issued by the union
in appreciation of King's cause. The union estimated
that in the 1960s it had raised more than $100,000 from
its members to support the southern freedom movement, and it would play a key role in the 1963 March on
Washington.*

---<><>---

Retail, Wholesale and Department Store Union (RWDSU) District 65
MONTICELLO, NEW YORK, SEPTEMBER 8, 1962

My good friend, President [David] Livingston, and to all of the members, all of the officers and friends of District 65, ladies and gentlemen. I need not pause to say how very delighted I am to have the opportunity of coming back to this beautiful setting, to be with you on the occasion of your convention. I never feel like a stranger or a visitor when I come among 65ers. I always feel at home and I always feel like one of you. For I can think of no labor union in the United States today that has given us the type of moral and financial support that you have given across these last few turbulent years. And this support has given us renewed courage and vigor to carry on in the struggle. I know we could not make it without this type of support.

Unfortunately, all labor unions affiliated with AFL-CIO are not as sensitive to the needs and not as concerned about the problems as District 65. It is refreshing indeed and encouraging to know that somebody still has the vision, the concern, the insight, and the moral commitment to realize that we are together, and that if the minority groups that are exploited and trampled over by the iron feet of oppression go up, labor will go up; and if we go down, labor will go down because the forces that are anti-Negro are anti-labor and vice versa. And therefore we must see that we are together in a struggle to make democracy a reality, and to make the American dream a reality in this day and this age.

But I want to talk with you about some of the problems we are facing in the world today and problems that we are facing in our own nation. And if I had to use a subject for the things that I would like to say to you I would use the subject "creative dissatisfaction."

There are three major social evils that are alive in our world today. And I would like to talk with you about these evils and urge each of you to maintain a keen sensitivity to these social evils that pervade our nation and our world. These three evils are the evil of war, the evil of economic injustice, and the evil of racial injustice.

And so that means that I start out saying that we must find some alternative to war. And God grant that we will come to see now that we can never again adjust to war and all of the evil consequences that result from war, for there is something at bottom evil about war. War stacks our nations with national debts higher than mountains of gold. War fills our nations with orphans and widows. War sends men home psychologically deranged and physically handicapped. And we've got to come to see now that there is something basically and fundamentally wrong with a world that seeks to solve its problems on the battlefield. . . .

In a day with Sputniks and Explorers dashing through outer space, and guided ballistic missiles carving highways of death through the stratosphere, no nation can win a war. It is no longer a choice between violence and non-violence, it is either nonviolence or nonexistence, and the alternative to disarmament, the alternative to suspension of nuclear tests, the alternative to strengthening the United Nations and thereby disarming the whole world, may well be a civilization plunged into the abyss of annihilation. War is evil, and there must be people all over this nation and all over this world, who will be a part of a creative minority, and who will develop a creative dissatisfaction where the whole question of war is concerned.

The other problem is one that you are very much familiar with; we all are. The problem is economic injustice. . . . We know that there is still in our world a great gulf between superfluous, inordinate wealth, and abject, deadening poverty. We see it in our nation and we see it in other nations. And we must always maintain a keen sensitivity to these conditions, for there is something wrong with a situation that will take the necessities from the masses and give luxuries to the classes.

Somehow, we are all caught in an inescapable network of mutuality tied in a single garment of destiny and we must see this over and over again. I think about the fact that right here in America, one-tenth of 1 percent of the population controls almost 50 percent of the wealth. Some changes must take place here, and I don't think the answer is in Communism, certainly not. Communism is based in ethical relativism, a metaphysical materialism, a denial of human freedom, and a totalitarianism that I can never accept. I believe that we can work within the framework of our democracy to make for a better distribution of wealth, and I believe that God has left enough and to spare in this world for all of his children to have the basic necessities of life. I will never be satisfied, and I will never be content, until all men and all women can have the basic necessities of life.

In the last two years I have done a little traveling in some of the other continents of our world, been in Africa, Asia, and South America, and in all of these countries and continents, I've noticed extreme poverty.

I said to myself, can we in America stand idly by and not be concerned? And something within cried out oh, no, because the destiny of the United States is tied up with the destiny of India. And somehow I had to think about the fact that right here in America, we spend more than a million dollars a day to store surplus food. I say to you this afternoon, that I know where we can store that food free of charge, in the wrinkled stomachs of the millions of people of Asia and Africa and South America.

Maybe we spend far too much of our national budget establishing military bases around the world rather than bases of genuine concern and understanding. All I'm saying is simply this: that all life is interrelated, and whatever affects one directly, affects all indirectly. John Donne was right in his poem, when he said, "No man is an island entire of itself: every man is a piece of the continent, a part of the main," and he goes on toward the end to say, "Any man's death diminishes me because I am involved in mankind. Therefore never send to know for whom the bell tolls; it tolls for thee."

The third evil is the evil of racial injustice. And again, we are all familiar with this. We have seen it in all of its ugly dimensions. We've seen it in the South. Legislative halls ring loud over such words as interposition and nullification. We've seen it in muddy Mississippi, crying out in the voice of little Emmett C. Till. We've seen it down in Leesburg, Georgia, where the church of God could be burned simply because people assembling in that church wanted to register and vote. We've seen it in Albany, Georgia. More than a thousand people have gone to jail, merely because they want to be free, and engage in peaceful protest, in order to make that freedom possible.

Yes, we've seen racial injustice, but not only have we seen it in the South. No section of our country can boast of clean hands in the area of brotherhood, and so we even see it in New York, in housing and employment discrimination. But I believe all of us are aware segregation must die. For segregation is a cancer in the body politic, which must be removed before our democratic and moral health can be realized.

We are challenged to work passionately and unrelentingly to get rid of this evil and unjust system. Now, of course, we need many agencies to work. We need the federal government to do something about it. The federal government has a great responsibility in this tense period of transition. This is why I've tried to get over to the president in the form of a document that there is a need now for the president of the United States to sign an executive order making it palpably clear that segregation is unconstitutional on the basis of the Fourteenth Amendment. This would be something of a second Emancipation Proclamation.

You will remember that almost one hundred years ago Abraham Lincoln signed the Emancipation Proclamation, which freed the Negro from the bondage of physical slavery. A hundred years later we still have slavery because segregation is nothing but slavery covered up with certain niceties of complexity. The time has come.

This is very important. Along with all that we do to get the federal government to act, we realize that if we are to be free, we must do something about it ourselves. For we have in our hands the creative, moral, nonviolent instruments to change the social situation. This is what we tried to emphasize in our struggle in the South. This is the meaning of the struggle taking place today in Albany, Georgia. This is what the people of Albany, Georgia, are saying: "We are determined to be free. And we have discovered a creative method, we have decided to stand up for that freedom, we have decided to suffer and sacrifice for that freedom."

We see in Albany, Georgia, the most vigorous determination to break down segregation to date, for all of the nonviolent methods are being used in Albany, for the first time and at the same time. Here you see sit-ins, stand-ins, wade-ins, kneel-ins, boycotts, working through the courts, and also working through the political area, by seeking to double the number of Negro registered voters. All of these are working together . . .

Three simple words explain the social revolution taking place in Albany and the South today. They aren't big words. One does not need to have a philosophical bent to understand them. They are three simple words: the word *all*, the word *here*, and the word *now*. [King's voice rises to a fevered pitch.] We don't want some of our rights. We don't want a few token handouts here and there. We want all of our rights, but we don't want to have to run anywhere else to get them, and so we will not join a back-to-Africa movement (Applause), nor will we take a one-way "freedom ride" ticket north sponsored by the White Citizens' Council movement. (Applause) What we are saying is that we want all of our rights and we want them here in the red hills of Georgia, here behind the cotton curtains of Alabama, here on the soils of Mississippi. We want all of our rights, and want them here! (Applause and cheering)

We aren't willing to wait two hundred years for our rights. No, we are not willing to wait one hundred and fifty years for our rights. We have lived with gradualism. And we know that gradualism is little more than a do-nothing-ism and an escapism which ends up in stand-stillism. And we are simply saying we want all of our rights, we want them here, and we want freedom now! This is what we want. (Applause and cheering)

In short, my friends, our goal is freedom. And I believe we will reach the goal because the goal of America is freedom. This is our destiny, and we are determined, and nothing can stop us.

But our destiny is tied up with the destiny of America. We worked right here two centuries without wages. We made cotton king. And we built our homes, and the homes of our masters, in the midst of injustice and humiliation. And yet, out of a bottomless vitality, we continue to grow and develop. And if the inexpressible cruelties of slavery couldn't stop us, certainly the opposition that we now face will not be able to stop us. And we will continue this struggle because we know that somehow the heritage of our nation and the will of God are somehow tied up in our echoing demands. And so we go on with this faith, and God grant that we together, all of the liberal forces, will move on toward that great day when the brotherhood of man will be a reality, when all of God's children will be able to join together, realizing that all men are significant and God's children, realizing that the basic thing about every man is his dignity and worth.

And if we will go on with that spirit we will be able to speed up that day when we will be able to sing with new meaning "My Country, 'Tis of Thee": "My country 'tis of thee, sweet land of liberty, of thee I sing. Land where our fathers died, land of the pilgrim's pride, from every mountainside let freedom ring." And that must become literally true all over this nation, and if we will make it true, we will be a great people, and we will be a great nation.

This is the challenge for people everywhere. This is the challenge for men of goodwill at this hour. This is the challenge of this moment. And may we do it with zeal and determination, not waiting until next year, not waiting until tomorrow morning, not waiting even an hour from now. Somewhere I read a little poem, which said, "A tiny little minute, just sixty seconds in it, I didn't choose it, I can't refuse it. It's up to me to use it. A tiny little minute, just sixty seconds in it, but eternity is in it." And if we will use the moment creatively and bring into being this new society, something will happen.

That will be the moment, figuratively speaking, when the morning stars will sing together and the sons of God will shout for joy. Thank you. (Applause)

VII

"Industry knows only two
types of workers who, in years
past, were brought frequently
to their jobs in chains."

N*ational Maritime Union (NMU) president Joseph Curran represented forty-five thousand seamen on the oceans, Great Lakes, and inland waterways. At a dinner that cost fifty dollars a plate and with fifteen hundred guests, Curran helped to raise $25,000 for King, the honorary president of the Gandhi Society for Human Rights, a New York group set up by his supporter to raise funds for the black freedom movement in the South. Curran had led the NMU since the 1930s alongside Secretary-Treasurer Ferdinand Smith, once the highest-ranking black union officer in the CIO. The union later shunned this remarkable Jamaican activist because he was a Communist, and the U.S. government deported him as an undesirable alien. During the Red Scare, Curran, who had previously allied with Communists in the union, sent thugs to beat up other presumed Communists purged (like King's lieutenant Hunter Pitts (Jack) O'Dell) from the NMU in the postwar years. In introducing King, Curran stressed that his union had placed anti-discrimination clauses in its contracts since 1944 and that "we have people of every color, black, yellow, white, and mixed." The union would never be satisfied until equality reigned, he said.*

The internal politics of the unions could be puzzling. King made an earlier similar fund-raising speech under the auspices of the Gandhi Society at a June 12, 1963, meeting hosted by Michael Quill, president of the Transport Workers Union (TWU). (King had also spoken to the TWU's eleventh constitutional convention in October 1961.) The fiery Irish American Quill, like Curran of the NMU, had once allied with Communists but spurned them during the Taft-Hartley Act and the Cold War. In 1962, a representative for King had also spoken to the United Electrical, Radio and Machine Workers Union (UE), the largest of the unions expelled from the CIO as "Communist-dominated." That union soldiered on with openly leftist leaders as other unions tried to raid its membership and destroy it.

Despite these internal conflicts within unions, even the most dedicated leftists often softened their political stance in order to promote their institutions, while union leaders from all over the political spectrum became increasingly militant equal rights advocates as the result of the civil rights upsurge. Even James Hoffa, president of the corrupted Teamsters union, supported King.

King began this speech to NMU members by noting the importance of interracial human solidarity to survival at sea and extrapolated from that the need for solidarity in upholding human rights for all people. He might have mentioned that the word strike came from the history of sailors who "struck" the topsails of merchant ships to protest bad labor conditions. King came to this speech six weeks after his release from jail in Albany, Georgia, where he experienced a frustrating year of arrests and mass demonstrations that produced few gains. Surely the labor history to which he refers in this speech must have seemed somewhat academic to King compared to the frightening business of organizing a movement in the South. King made hundreds of speeches every year, switching back and forth from jail and street marches in blue jeans to banquet halls with men in white shirts. He couldn't possibly have known enough to write speeches that fit the various unions; his first rough draft sometimes came from his union-wise supporters in New York City. These efforts nonetheless helped King to develop political solidarity with unions that also provided some of his strongest financial support.

---◇◆◇---

National Maritime Union
NEW YORK CITY, OCTOBER 23, 1962

Industry knows only two types of workers who, in years past, were brought frequently to their job in chains— Negroes and shanghaied seamen. In those days only these workers were physically bound to their place of employment—the Negro to his plantation by guards, and the seaman by the watery isolation of his ship. Yours was never as humiliating a condition as chattel slavery, but the abuse of your freedom, and dignity of personality, were corrosive and destructive.

The sailors wrote a luminous page of history when they used their mighty strength and unity to civilize their work conditions. Everyone benefitted—other labor groups as well as employers because the violence and instability of the sea life of old could not be a basis for a great commerce. Nor could maltreated, brutalized men be entrusted with the multimillion-dollar ships of the modern era; nor with the safety of millions of passengers who now make the seas a highway.

And so you and your industry have come a long way from great depths to great heights in your journey, achieving democratic practices which put you above many other segments of American life.

What do I mean by this? I believe there is more simple nobility in your work than in almost any other. First, in the progress toward integration you are matchless because an integrated ship is a flower of democracy. On the sea, workers not only toil side by side, but they eat, sleep, and relax on an integrated basis. You are not divided by color, religion, or other distinctions. The men of a department work and sleep and eat without artificially imposed barriers between them. Mastering nature's giant seas requires unity, brotherhood, and in moments of peril, the *color* of a man's skin is of no importance, but the *quality* of his courage and resourcefulness is all important.

Sailors are unique workers possessing noble qualities because in time of war they assume risks many soldiers never experience, even though they remain civilians.

Lastly, every sailor is expected in the tradition of the sea to be willing to risk his life in order to save the life of another.

Some years ago I read a newspaper story of an American liner which altered its course and stood by in a storm because a single man had been sighted floating on a raft. Thousands of passengers, many of them leaders of industry and eminent statesmen, were compelled to wait— perhaps altering a thousand appointments and conferences. The delivery of cargo and mail were delayed until one man was rescued from death. For me this incident had overwhelming spiritual and moral meaning because the multitude of distinguished people, who were inconvenienced, and the fortune in wealth which waited upon one man, dramatized the importance of a single human being in an age when we too easily forget people. But this incident was multiplied in meaning because that one man, whose life hung in the balance, was discovered to be a Negro when the lifeboat brought him to safety.

It is not often that everything stops and holds its breath for an ordinary Negro. I am happy to say that a similar situation finally did occur on land only recently when the governor of Mississippi tried to reverse history and victimize one Negro, only to find hundreds of millions lining up with James Meredith and an army mobilized at his side, for the sole purpose of ensuring his rights as an American citizen.

Reaching far back into the past, it is interesting that the brutal practice of flogging on ships was fought and abolished by a member of another minority group in the eighteenth century when Commodore Uriah Levy, a Jew, ended this barbaric practice in the U.S. Navy.

All of your progress in humanism spread to other sectors of American life, making you pioneers of the human spirit.

So it is a natural extension of your tradition, it is consistent with your sense of brotherhood, that in celebrating your twenty-fifth anniversary, that with your deserved enjoyment and delight in the event, you also use it to make financial aid available to a people still fighting to realize their elementary rights and still seeking the long-promised pursuit of happiness. Your twenty-fifth anniversary arranged in this constructive fashion honors you even beyond the achievement of twenty-five years of organized life. You sum up thousands of years of man's struggle to be human, decent, and honorable.

Our nation is facing severe trials in these turbulent days because one region of our country still holds itself above law, as if it were cut adrift from constitutional obligations, and insurrection and mutiny against the government is still possible. They not only abuse persons, but they debase the democratic traditions of the nation in their defiant resort to anarchy and storm troop rule.

Against this force, which has the power of states at its command, Negroes have searched for effective weapons. We believe we have found them. Emulating the labor movement, we in the South have embraced mass actions— boycotts, sit-ins and, more recently, a widespread utilization of the ballot.

Emulating Biblical teachers and Mahatma Gandhi, we have seized the unique weapon of nonviolent resistance.

It is a pleasure to tell you that our weapons work. They do not draw the blood of our adversary, but they do defeat the unjust system.

A remarkably effective method has evolved and become a source of splendid strength in recent months. The secret ballot is our secret weapon.

In the state of Georgia a quiet revolution is taking place. My organization, the Southern Christian Leadership Conference, has been persistently carrying on a voting and registration drive in concert with other groups. First in Atlanta, the Negro vote joined with white allies casting our ballots in secret, and together we crushed a rabid segregationist and put into the mayoralty seat a white moderate, who has already with us broken more walls of segregation in a year than were destroyed in decades. . . . [King went on to cite political victories in his home state of Georgia based on registering black voters, leading to the election of more moderate candidates for governor and Congress.]

It is heartwarming to share your successes, and gratifying to tell you of ours. We still have a long way to go and if we forget how great the sacrifices will be, there are always arsonists, lunatics, and rampaging bigots to remind us that death lurks nearby. But if physical death is the price that we must pay to free our children and our white children from a permanent death of the spirit, we'll accept it with quiet courage . . .

Our lives are an endless concert of tensions, struggle, and pain. Many who would speak are silent. I have often looked at the imposing, segregated churches, which the religious South has in profusion, and asked the troubling question, "What kind of people worship there? Who is their God?"

I don't know what kind of church you worship in. Perhaps many of you worship in none. Yet I know what kind of people you are and I know what God you worship.

In your long struggle for humanity and justice, you are religious in the deepest sense, whether you have realized it or not.

With all our problems we are optimistic. We are presiding over a dying order, one which has long deserved to die. We operate in stormy seas, but I often remember some beautiful words of Eugene Debs to the court which imprisoned him for his pacifism:

I can see the dawn of a better humanity. The people are awakening. In due course of time they will come to their own.

When the mariner, sailing over tropic seas, looks for relief from his weary watch, he turns his eye toward the Southern Cross, burning luridly above the tempest-vexed ocean. As the midnight approaches, the southern cross begins to bend, and the whirling-worlds change their places, and with starry finger-points the Almighty marks the passage of time upon the dial of the universe, and though no bell may bear the glad tidings, the lookout knows that the midnight is passing—that relief and rest are close at hand.

Let the people take heart and hope everywhere, for the cross is bending, the midnight is passing, and joy cometh with the morning.

VIII

"Now is the time to make real the promises of democracy."

K ing linked the issues of racism and discrimination to the problem of economic injustice with indelible word portraits. At the great March on Washington on August 28, 1963, King declared that, one hundred years since the Emancipation Proclamation, the African American still "lives on a lonely island of poverty in the midst of a vast ocean of material prosperity . . . an exile in his own land." The nation had defaulted on its promissory note of equal rights for all with a bounced check that came back marked "insufficient funds." (In other speeches he explained that the U.S. had declared freedom but hadn't given former slaves land and left freed people stranded in the South and in northern slums without sufficient jobs, education, and income.) King at the March on Washington departed from his text to build to an emotional crescendo, inspiring Americans to live up to the nation's greatest promises and using the "I have a dream" metaphor to capture the nation's image of its place in history as a place of freedom.

Most people watching King's brilliant speech today don't know that the March on Washington originated as a labor march or that King had given a very similar ex-

hortation six weeks earlier in Detroit and had used the "I have a dream" phrase numerous times before. In a prelude to the March on Washington on June 23, 125,000 to 150,000 people filled a twenty-one-block area after marching down Woodward Avenue in Detroit, a city dense with workers in auto assembly and supply plants. It was not a labor march, but it was supported by the UAW and other unions and it played out in the context of the city's long-standing racial and labor issues. This march marked a twenty-year anniversary of an event during World War II, when a bloody white race riot against black working-class immigrants had left thirty-four people dead and seven hundred injured. The march sought to banish that legacy of racial and labor conflict as well as to hold up King's campaign to get the president to issue a new Emancipation Proclamation to end segregation and disenfranchisement. It took place only twelve days after the assassination of NAACP leader Medgar Evers in Mississippi, and in the wake of the tumultuous demonstrations for freedom in Birmingham. In contrast to the deep South, in Detroit, Reverend Clarence L. Franklin, pastor of the New Bethel Baptist Church and chairman of the Council for Human Rights, joined black church members with white participants like the UAW's Walter Reuther, the city's mayor, Jerome Cavanaugh, and even the former governor of Michigan, John B. Swainson, to demand "freedom now." Reverend Albert Cleague, an early proponent of black power, also spoke.

Unions played the role of a junior partner to the black church in this coalition, but the Detroit march nonetheless cemented an alliance between King and the UAW that would help to produce the most tangible results of the southern freedom movement, the Civil Rights Act of 1964 and the Voting Rights Act of 1965. The UAW had *supported the Montgomery Bus Boycott in 1956, bailed freedom riders out of jail in 1961, and, during a crucial moment in spring 1963, Reuther raised $160,000 from unions to get protestors out of jail in Birmingham. No one but "big labor" could offer such support. Reuther joined King as a keynote speaker at the Detroit march, and not long after Reuther and the UAW would bring trainloads, busloads, and even planeloads of people to the March on Washington. The union had a powerful Washington office that helped to defeat filibuster threats in the U.S. Senate in order to pass civil rights laws. Reuther and the UAW organized key constituents in legislative districts in crucial Midwest states like Michigan to pass not only the Civil Rights and Voting Rights acts but a raft of other legislation for Medicare, Medicaid, and programs to end poverty. (In a less salutary use of his economic power, however, Reuther threatened King with a loss of funding if he refused to accept an unsavory compromise in response to the Mississippi Freedom Democratic Party's challenge to an all-white delegation from that state at the 1964 Democratic National Convention.)*

King opened this speech at the Detroit Freedom March by calling it "the largest and greatest demonstration for freedom ever held in the United States," but two months later the March on Washington would take that prize. Notable here is King's warning to Detroiters that one of the best ways to support the southern freedom movement would be to end housing, school, and job discrimination in Detroit. King used his "I have a dream" metaphor in Detroit to bring his speech to an inspiring crescendo, and he included this line: "I have a dream this afternoon that one day right here in Detroit, Negroes will be able to buy a house and rent a house anywhere that their money will carry them and they will be able to get a job." The Detroit

march in a real way helped to cement a national labor–
civil rights coalition that ultimately broke the back of Jim
Crow. But failure to overturn discrimination, police bru-
tality, and unemployment in Motor City would lead to
the worst race riot of the 1960s in the summer of 1967.
The destructive effects of automation and right-wing as-
saults that King warned about so often would continue to
shred the job base for autoworkers and whittle the UAW
down to a small fraction of its former self.

———◇◇◇———

Detroit March for Civil Rights
DETROIT, MICHIGAN, JUNE 23, 1963

My good friend, the Reverend C. L. Franklin, and all of
the officers and members of the Detroit Council of Human
Rights, distinguished platform guests, ladies and gentlemen. I cannot begin to say to you this afternoon how
thrilled I am. And I cannot begin to tell you the deep joy
that comes to my heart as I participate with you in what
I consider the largest and greatest demonstration for freedom ever held in the United States.

And I can assure you that what has been done here
today will serve as a source of inspiration for all of the
freedom-loving people of this nation.

I think there is something else that must be said because it is a magnificent demonstration of discipline. With
all of the thousands and hundreds of thousands of people
engaged in this demonstration today, Commissioner Ed-
wards reports to me that there has not been one reported
incidence of violence. I think this is a magnificent demonstration of our commitment to nonviolence in this struggle
for freedom all over the U.S., and I want to commend the
leadership of this community for making this great event

possible and making such a great event possible through such disciplined channels.

Almost 101 years ago, on September the twenty-second, 1862, to be exact, a great and noble American, Abraham Lincoln, signed an executive order, which was to take effect on January the first, 1863. This executive order was called the Emancipation Proclamation and it served to free the Negro from the bondage of physical slavery. But one hundred years later, the Negro in the United States of America still isn't free. (Applause)

But now more than ever before, America is forced to grapple with this problem, for the shape of the world today does not afford us the luxury of an anemic democracy. The price that this nation must pay for the continued oppression and exploitation of the Negro or any other minority group is the price of its own destruction. For the hour is late. The clock of destiny is ticking out, and we must act now before it is too late. (Yeah) (Applause)

The events of Birmingham, Alabama, and the more than sixty communities that have started protest movements since Birmingham, are indicative of the fact that the Negro is now determined to be free. (Yeah) (Applause) For Birmingham tells us something in glaring terms. It says first that the Negro is no longer willing to accept racial segregation in any of its dimensions. (Applause) For we have come to see that segregation is not only sociologically untenable, it is not only politically unsound, it is morally wrong and sinful. Segregation is a cancer in the body politic, which must be removed before our democratic health can be realized. (Applause) (Yeah) Segregation is wrong because it is nothing but a new form of slavery covered up with certain niceties of complexity. (Applause) Segregation is wrong because it is a system of adultery perpetuated by an illicit intercourse between injustice and immorality. (Applause) And in Birmingham, Alabama, and all over the

South and all over the nation, we are simply saying that we will no longer sell our birthright of freedom for a mess of segregated pottage. (Applause) (All right) In a real sense, we are through with segregation now, henceforth, and forevermore. (Sustained applause)

Now Birmingham and the freedom struggle tell us something else. They reveal to us that the Negro has a new sense of dignity and a new sense of self-respect. (Yes) For years—(That's right. Come a long way) (Applause)—I think we all will agree that probably the most damaging effect of segregation has been what it has done to the soul of the segregated as well as the segregator. (Applause) It has given the segregator a false sense of superiority, and it has left the segregated with a false sense of inferiority. (All right) (Applause) And so because of the legacy of slavery and segregation, many Negroes lost faith in themselves and many felt that they were inferior.

But then something happened to the Negro. Circumstances made it possible and necessary for him to travel more: the coming of the automobile, the upheavals of two world wars, the Great Depression. And so his rural, plantation background gradually gave way to urban, industrial life. And even his economic life was rising through the growth of industry, the influence of organized labor, expanded educational opportunities. And even his cultural life was rising through the steady decline of crippling illiteracy. And all of these forces conjoined to cause the Negro to take a new look at himself. Negro masses, (Applause) Negro masses all over began to reevaluate themselves, and the Negro came to feel that he was somebody. His religion revealed to him, (Laughter and applause) his religion revealed to him that God loves all of His children, and that all men are made in His image, and that figuratively speaking, every man from a bass-black to a treble-white is significant on God's keyboard. (Applause)

So, the Negro can now unconsciously cry out with the eloquent poet:

> Fleecy locks and black complexion
> Cannot forfeit nature's claim.
> Skin may differ, but affection
> Dwells in black and white the same.
> Were I so tall as to reach the pole
> Or to grasp at the ocean at a span,
> I must be measured by my soul
> The mind is the standard of the man. (Applause)

But these events that are taking place in our nation tell us something else. They tell us that the Negro and his allies in the white community now recognize the urgency of the moment. I know we have heard a lot of cries saying, "Slow up and cool off." (Laughter) We still hear these cries. They are telling us over and over again that you're pushing things too fast, and so they're saying, "Cool off." Well, the only answer that we can give to that is that we've cooled off all too long, and that is the danger. (Applause) There's always the danger if you cool off too much that you will end up in a deep freeze. (Applause) "Well," they're saying, "you need to put on brakes." The only answer that we can give to that is that the motor's now cranked up and we're moving up the highway of freedom toward the city of equality, (Applause) and we can't afford to stop now because our nation has a date with destiny. We must keep moving.

Then there is another cry. They say, "Why don't you do it in a gradual manner?" Well, gradualism is little more than escapism and do-nothingism, which ends up in standstillism. (Applause) We know that our brothers and sisters in Africa and Asia are moving with jetlike speed toward the goal of political independence. And in some communities we are still moving at a horse-and-buggy pace toward the gaining of a hamburger and a cup of coffee at a lunch counter. (Applause)

And so we must say, now is the time to make real the promises of democracy. Now is the time to transform this pending national elegy into a creative psalm of brotherhood. Now is the time to lift our nation. (Applause) Now is the time to lift our nation from the quicksands of racial injustice to the solid rock of racial justice. Now is the time to get rid of segregation and discrimination. Now is the time. (Applause) (Now, now)

And so this social revolution taking place can be summarized in three little words. They are not big words. One does not need an extensive vocabulary to understand them. They are the words *all*, *here*, and *now*. We want *all* of our rights, we want them *here*, and we want them *now*. (Applause) This is the meaning. (Applause) . . . [Recording interrupted.]

Now the other thing that we must see about this struggle is that by and large it has been a nonviolent struggle. Let nobody make you feel that those who are engaged or who are engaging in the demonstrations in communities all across the South are resorting to violence; these are few in number. For we've come to see the power of nonviolence. We've come to see that this method is not a weak method, for it's the strong man who can stand up amid opposition, who can stand up amid violence being inflicted upon him and not retaliate with violence. (Yeah) (Applause)

You see, this method has a way of disarming the opponent. It exposes his moral defenses. It weakens his morale, and at the same time it works on his conscience, and he just doesn't know what to do. If he doesn't beat you, wonderful. If he beats you, you develop the quiet courage of accepting blows without retaliating. If he doesn't put you in jail, wonderful. Nobody with any sense likes to go to

jail. But if he puts you in jail, you go in that jail and transform it from a dungeon of shame to a haven of freedom
and human dignity. (Applause) And even if he tries to kill
you, (He can't kill you) you'll develop the inner conviction
that there are some things so dear, some things so pre-
cious, some things so eternally true, that they are worth
dying for. (Yes) (Applause) And I submit to you that if a
man has not discovered something that he will die for, he
isn't fit to live. (Applause)

This method has wrought wonders. As a result of the
nonviolent freedom ride movement, segregation in public
transportation has almost passed away absolutely in the
South. As a result of the sit-in movement at lunch counters, more than 285 cities have now integrated their lunch
counters in the South. I say to you, there is power in this
method. (Applause)

And I think by following this approach it will also help
us to go into the new age that is emerging with the right at-
titude. For nonviolence not only calls upon its adherents to
avoid external physical violence, but it calls upon them
to avoid internal violence of spirit. It calls on them to engage in that something called love. And I know it is difficult
sometimes. When I say "love" at this point, I'm not talking
about an affectionate emotion. (All right) It's nonsense to
urge people, oppressed people, to love their oppressors in
an affectionate sense. I'm talking about something much
deeper. I'm talking about a sort of understanding, creative,
redemptive goodwill for all men. (Applause)

We are coming to see now, the psychiatrists are saying to us, that many of the strange things that happen in
the subconscious, many of the inner conflicts, are rooted
in hate. And so they are saying, "Love or perish." But
Jesus told us this a long time ago. And I can still hear
that voice crying through the vista of time, saying, "Love
your enemies, bless them that curse you, pray for them

that despitefully use you." And there is still a voice saying to every potential Peter, "Put up your sword." History is replete with the bleached bones of nations, history is cluttered with the wreckage of communities that failed to follow this command. And isn't it marvelous to have a method of struggle where it is possible to stand up against an unjust system, fight it with all of your might, never accept it, and yet not stoop to violence and hatred in the process? This is what we have. (Applause)

Now there is a magnificent new militancy within the Negro community all across this nation. And I welcome this as a marvelous development. The Negro of America is saying he's determined to be free and he is militant enough to stand up. But this new militancy must not lead us to the position of distrusting every white person who lives in the United States. There are some white people in this country who are as determined to see the Negro free as we are to be free. (Applause) This new militancy must be kept within understanding boundaries.

And then another thing I can understand. We've been pushed around so long; we've been the victims of lynching mobs so long; we've been the victims of economic injustice so long—still the last hired and the first fired all over this nation. And I know the temptation. I can understand from a psychological point of view why some caught up in the clutches of the injustices surrounding them almost respond with bitterness and come to the conclusion that the problem can't be solved within, and they talk about getting away from it in terms of racial separation. But even though I can understand it psychologically, I must say to you this afternoon that this isn't the way. Black supremacy is as dangerous as white supremacy. (Applause) No, I hope you will allow me to say to you this afternoon that God is not interested merely in the freedom of black men and brown men and yellow men. God is interested in the freedom of the whole human race. (Applause) And I believe that with this philosophy and this determined struggle we will be able to go on in the days ahead and transform the jangling discords of our nation into a beautiful symphony of brotherhood.

As I move toward my conclusion, you're asking, I'm sure, "What can we do here in Detroit to help in the struggle in the South?" Well, there are several things that you can do. One of them you've done already, and I hope you will do it in even greater dimensions before we leave this meeting. . . . [Recording interrupted.]

Now the second thing that you can do to help us down in Alabama and Mississippi and all over the South is to work with determination to get rid of any segregation and discrimination in Detroit, (Applause) realizing that injustice anywhere is a threat to justice everywhere. And we've got to come to see that the problem of racial injustice is a national problem. No community in this country can boast of clean hands in the area of brotherhood. Now in the North it's different in that it doesn't have the legal sanction that it has in the South. But it has its subtle and hidden forms and it exists in three areas: in the area of employment discrimination, in the area of housing discrimination, and in the area of de facto segregation in the public schools. And we must come to see that de facto segregation in the North is just as injurious as the actual segregation in the South. (Applause) And so if you want to help us in Alabama and Mississippi and over the South, do all that you can to get rid of the problem here.

And then we also need your support in order to get the civil rights bill that the president is offering passed. And there's a reality, let's not fool ourselves: this bill isn't going to get through if we don't put some work in it and some determined pressure. And this is why I've said that in order to get this bill through, we've got to arouse the conscience of the nation, and we ought to march to Washington more than one hundred thousand in order to say, (Applause) in order to say that we are determined, and in order to engage in a nonviolent protest to keep this issue before the conscience of the nation.

And if we will do this we will be able to bring that new day of freedom into being. If we will do this we will be able to make the American dream a reality. And I do not want to give you the impression that it's going to be easy. There can be no great social gain without individual pain. And before the victory for brotherhood is won, some will have to get scarred up a bit. Before the victory is won, some more will be thrown into jail. Before the victory is won, some, like Medgar Evers, may have to face physical death. But if physical death is the price that some must pay to free their children and their white brothers from an eternal psychological death, then nothing can be more redemptive. Before the victory is won, some will be misunderstood and called bad names, but we must go on with a determination and with a faith that this problem can be solved. (Yeah) (Applause)

And so I go back to the South not in despair. I go back to the South not with a feeling that we are caught in a dark dungeon that will never lead to a way out. I go back believing that the new day is coming. And so this afternoon, I have a dream. (Go ahead) It is a dream deeply rooted in the American dream.

I have a dream that one day, right down in Georgia and Mississippi and Alabama, the sons of former slaves and the sons of former slave owners will be able to live together as brothers.

I have a dream this afternoon (I have a dream) that one day, (Applause) one day little white children and little Negro children will be able to join hands as brothers and sisters.

I have a dream this afternoon that one day, (Applause) that one day men will no longer burn down houses and the church of God simply because people want to be free.

I have a dream this afternoon (I have a dream) that there will be a day that we will no longer face the atrocities that Emmett Till had to face or Medgar Evers had to face, that all men can live with dignity.

I have a dream this afternoon (Yeah) that my four little children, that my four little children will not come up in the same young days that I came up within, but they will be judged on the basis of the content of their character, not the color of their skin. (Applause)

I have a dream this afternoon that one day, right here in Detroit, Negroes will be able to buy a house or rent a house anywhere that their money will carry them and they will be able to get a job. (Applause) (That's right)

Yes, I have a dream this afternoon that one day in this land the words of Amos will become real and "justice will roll down like waters and righteousness like a mighty stream."

I have a dream this evening that one day we will recognize the words of Jefferson that "all men are created equal, that they are endowed by their creator with certain unalienable rights, that among these are life, liberty, and the pursuit of happiness." I have a dream this afternoon. (Applause)

I have a dream that one day "every valley shall be exalted, and every hill shall be made low; the crooked places shall be made straight, and the rough places plain; and the glory of the Lord shall be revealed, and all flesh shall see it together." (Applause)

I have a dream this afternoon that the brotherhood of man will become a reality in this day.

And with this faith I will go out and carve a tunnel of hope through the mountain of despair. With this faith,

I will go out with you and transform dark yesterdays into bright tomorrows. With this faith, we will be able to achieve this new day when all of God's children, black men and white men, Jews and Gentiles, Protestants and Catholics, will be able to join hands and sing with the Negroes in the spiritual of old:

> Free at last! Free at last!
> Thank God Almighty, we are free at last!

(Applause)

IX

"The unresolved race question"

For a year leading up to the one-hundredth anniversary, in 1963, of President Abraham Lincoln's Emancipation Proclamation freeing of the slaves, King campaigned to get President John F. Kennedy to declare a second Emancipation Proclamation and issue an executive order enforcing civil rights and voting rights. Fearful of segregationist southern Democrats and northern Republicans who controlled committees of Congress and threatened to filibuster any progressive legislation, Kennedy did nothing until King and others organized a mass movement in Birmingham, Alabama, that triggered desegregation struggles throughout the South and led to the hugely effective March on Washington. Those events forced Kennedy to demand a civil rights law.

King in his previous speech at District 65 had promised to attend its thirtieth annual convention on the understanding that it would also use that occasion to celebrate the Emancipation Proclamation. District 65 secretary-treasurer Cleveland Robinson had handled much financing and organizing for the March on Washington and remained one of King's closest labor advisors.

Up to twenty thousand people appeared on October 23 at Madison Square Garden in New York City, as did the Mayor Robert Wagner, all celebrating the thirtieth anniversary of the union and the one-hundredth anniversary of the Emancipation Proclamation. This massive event created huge excitement and contributed to raising $100,000 for a Freedom Fund that it created through repeated contributions by union members, one dollar at a time.

This speech followed not only the immense success of the March on Washington but also the murder of Medgar Evers in the summer and then the horrendous bombing of the 16th Street Baptist Church that killed four girls in Birmingham. King told the New York Times *that mass rallies and organizing set off by the Birmingham movement and the March on Washington had infused African Americans in the North with a new militancy but had also raised violent resentments among some whites. One of his most ardent supporters in the North remained District 65, which consisted largely of African Americans and Puerto Ricans led by veterans of New York City's old labor left. Cleveland Robinson served on the SCLC board and would continue to push labor issues there throughout the 1960s. He also helped to organize a ticker-tape parade for King when he returned from Oslo, Norway, after receiving the Nobel Peace Prize in December 1964.*

This speech is drawn from a transcript in the King files in Atlanta supplemented by a District 65 recording issued as an album to union members. King begins the speech in a quiet and sober way but builds up to the kind of crescendo for which he was so well known.

District 65

NEW YORK CITY, OCTOBER 23, 1963

My dear friend, David Livingston; to the distinguished mayor of this city; distinguished platform guests; members of District 65; ladies and gentlemen.

First, let me warmly commend you on this your thirtieth anniversary observance. In the years of your existence you have had continual growth. Against many massive international unions, you may be numerically small; you are small, however, only in one dimension. When we look deeply into your quality, you are like a diamond in a massive vein of coal. You could have allowed the stability and strength you accumulated to desensitize you to the burning problems of the less fortunate. You could have made respectability your main concern. You could have encased your fighting tradition in a plastic frame and hung it on your wall. Instead, you have brought your luminous tradition into the present, and wherever a battle for decency is waging, you have made yourself part of it.

We in the Southern Christian Leadership Conference will remain eternally indebted to you for your great moral and financial support. I can say without fear of successful contradiction that no labor union in this country has given us as much consistent and loyal support as you have. (Applause) There may be bigger unions than you and bigger treasuries but there is none whose heart and conscience is larger. (Applause) And in a day when all too many trade unions have lost the vibrant idealism that they possessed in the thirties, District 65 stands as a refreshing ray of hope. Indeed, you are the conscience of the labor movement. (Applause) When the day comes that your example becomes the theme of the whole trade union movement, the brotherhood of which men have dreamed will begin to live in the real world around us.

I'd like to take just a moment to thank you for the recent help and encouragement that you have given us in our struggle in Birmingham, Alabama. This has been a difficult struggle, but may I assure you that we are still on the job. Our epic fight was powerful enough to retire Bull Connor from the public life. (Applause) That alone was a victory for justice. And our fight was powerful enough to split apart the barrier that confined us in a prison on one side of the city. It was powerful enough to enable us to wrest some tokens of dignity from unwilling hands.

Most of all, it was powerful enough for us to learn how to win battles and how to wage new ones, until all our demands are fulfilled. Unfortunately, it was not powerful enough to permit us to say we have won everything in an irrevocable victory. We are still in the trenches in Birmingham because the economic and political power structure will give us no more, give up no more easily to us than they gave up to the unions when they sought to organize years ago. Just as they made concessions to the unions and continued to fight to hold down wage rates, they are trying to give to us with one hand and snatch back with the other every gain we make. But hard though they fight, they must lose in the end. The Negroes of Birmingham are not the same people they were seven months ago. Not only are they changed, but much in the South has changed. (Enthusiastic applause)

Now as we think of this significant occasion commemorating the centennial of the Emancipation Proclamation, may I say that mankind through the ages has been in a ceaseless struggle to give dignity and meaning to human life. If our nation had done nothing more in its whole history [than] to create just two documents, its contribution to civilization would be imperishable. The first of these documents is the Declaration of Independence, and the other is that which we are here tonight to honor, the Emancipation Proclamation. All tyrants past, present, and future are powerless to bury the truths in these documents, no matter how extensive their legions, how vast their power, and how malignant their evil.

The Declaration of Independence proclaimed to a world organized politically and spiritually around the concept of the inequality of man, that the liberty and dignity of human personality were inherent in man as a living being. The Emancipation Proclamation was the offspring of the Declaration of Independence, using the forces of law to uproot a social order which sought to separate liberty from a segment of humanity. Our pride and our progress could be unqualified if the story might end here. But history reveals that these documents were each to live lives of stormy contradictions, to be both observed and violated through social upheavals and spiritual disasters.

If we look at our history with honesty and clarity we will be forced to admit that our federal form of government has been, from the day of its birth, weakened in integrity, confused and confounded in its direction, by the unresolved race question.

It is as if a political thalidomide drug taken during pregnancy caused the birth of a crippled nation. Our nation has experienced a ceaseless rebellion against the Declaration of Independence, the Constitution, the Emancipation Proclamation, and the Supreme Court, by one region. In the Revolutionary War, powerful slave elements in the South fought with the British; the development of the nation to the West was complicated and hindered by the slave power. Although the holocaust of war settled the direction and character of our growth, the rebellion against equality continued into the second half of the nineteenth century, and into the twentieth century, diminishing the authority of the federal government and corroding its power. It has contaminated every institution in our society, in every year of our existence.

Still today, that single region of our county holds the veto power over the majority of our nation, nullifying basic constitutional rights, and in the exercise of its illegal conduct, retarding our growth. The South is an autonomous region whose posture toward the central government has elements as defiant as a hostile nation. Only the undeveloped nations of the world tolerate regions which are similar; it is a condition unknown to modern, industrial societies, except for our own.

And so the unresolved race question is a pathological infection in our social and political anatomy, which has sickened us throughout our history. How has our social health been injured by this condition? The legacy [is] the impairment of the lives of twenty million of our citizens, based solely on their color. They have been condemned to a subexistence, never sharing the fruits of progress equally. The average Negro, the average income of Negroes is approximately $3,300 per family annually, against $5,800 for white citizens. This differential tells only one part of the story. The more terrible aspect is found in the inner structure and quality of the Negro community. It is a community artificially, but effectively, separated from the dominant culture of our society. Every Negro knows these truths, and his personality is corroded by a sense of inferiority, generated by this degraded status. Negroes North and South still live in segregation, housed in slums, eat in segregation, pray in segregation, and die in segregation. The imposition of inferiority, externally and internally, are the slave chains of today.

And inequality before the law is so pervasive in the life of the Negro that its detailing is impossible. We boast that ours is a government of laws, but every Negro knows a thousand examples in which law and government do not protect him. In the past weeks Christian churches were bombed and innocent, unoffending children were brutally murdered in Birmingham, Alabama. If a government building were bombed in Washington, the perpetrators would be shot down in the streets, but if violence (Applause), but if violence affects the life or property of a Negro, not all the agencies of government can find or convict the murderers. . . .

This is the essential texture (Applause) of freedom and equality for the Negro one hundred years after the Emancipation Proclamation, and 186 years after the Declaration of Independence.

This somber picture may induce the somber thought that there is nothing to commemorate about the centennial of the Emancipation Proclamation, but tragic disappointments and undeserved defeats do not put an end to life, nor do they wipe out the positive, however submerged it may have become beneath the floods of negative experience. The Emancipation Proclamation had four enduring results: First, it gave force to the executive power to change conditions in the national interest on a broad and far-reaching scale. Second, it dealt a devastating blow to a system of slaveholding and an economy based upon it. Third, it enabled the Negro to play a significant role in his own liberation with the ability to organize and to struggle. Fourth, it resurrected and restored the principle of equality upon which the founding of the nation rested. When Abraham Lincoln signed the Emancipation Proclamation, it was not the act of an opportunistic politician issuing a hollow pronouncement to placate a pressure group. Only truly great presidents, all of our true great presidents, were tortured deep in their hearts by the race question.

Jefferson with keen perception saw that the immorality of slavery degraded the white master as well as the

Negro. He feared for the future of white children who were taught a false supremacy. His concern can be summed up in one quotation, "I tremble for my country when I reflect that God is just." Lincoln's torments are well known; his vacillations were fact. In the seething cauldron of '62 and '63, Lincoln was called the baboon president in the North, and coward, assassin, savage, murderer of babies in the South. Yet he searched his way to the conclusion embodied in these words: "In giving freedom to the slave, we assure freedom to the free." And on this moral foundation he personally prepared the first draft of the Emancipation Proclamation. Lincoln achieved immortality because he issued this proclamation. His hesitation had not stayed his hand. When historic necessity charted but one course, no president can be great, or even fit for office if he attempts to accommodate to injustice to maintain his political image. (Applause)

There is but one way to commemorate the Emancipation Proclamation, and that is to make its declaration of freedom real, to reach back to the origins of our nation, when our message of equality electrified an unfree world, and reaffirm democracy by deeds as bold and daring as the issuance of the Emancipation Proclamation. We do not have as much time as the cautious and the patient try to give us. We are not only living in a time of cataclysmic change; we live in an era in which human rights is the central world issue. A totally new political phenomenon has arisen from the rubble and destruction of World War II. A neutralist sector has established itself between the two contending camps of the world. More than a billion people are in the neutralist arena, and it is growing everywhere, even in the Western Hemisphere, covering territory larger than our national boundaries. These nations are neutral because they do not trust the integrity of the East or West in the issue of equality and human rights. (Applause)

Our declarations that we are making progress in race relations ring with pathetic emptiness in their ears. In India, Indonesia, Ghana, and Brazil, to mention but a few states which contain almost a billion humans, the right to vote has been exercised even by illiterate peasants in primitive villages. In some of our glittering cities in the South, college professors cannot vote, cannot eat, and cannot use the library or a park in equality. In Africa, Negroes have formed states and governed themselves and functioned in world tribunals with dignity and effectiveness. The simple fact is that the relative progress in undeveloped sectors of the world in human rights races at jet speed while we strain in a horse-and-buggy for advancement. (Applause) We are not moving in the world tempo of change; we're still, as the earth shrinks through communication revolutions. As the shame of Oxford, Mississippi, and Birmingham, Alabama, flashes around the globe, the world is becoming aware of our deficiencies.

Floods of consumer goods, superhighways, supermarkets, and Telstars [satellites] do not obscure the existence of shameful prejudice. And this fact, more than any other, explains why more emerging nations move away from us than toward us. Without the faith, (Applause), without the faith that we are wedded to great truths of equality and justice, our power and strength becomes a menace to other peoples, and they will maintain their distance until we have justified their confidence. The Negro will never cease his struggle to commemorate the Emancipation Proclamation by making his emancipation real. If enough Americans in number and influence join him, the nation we both labor to build may yet realize its glorious dream.

And it is important for you as trade unionists to know that we are not going to settle for less than full victory because one part of our struggle merges with a substantial fight which is at the top of your agenda. Millions of people are jobless, even while business leaders complacently and contentedly announce that our economy is robust.

You and I cannot win our fight for a decent life, unless we cope with the emerging threat of automation. It is already grinding into dust your jobs, and ours. It has kept unemployment at a high level, despite spectacular increases in production. Millions of people are jobless, even while business leaders are complacently and contentedly pronouncing the economy as surging and robust. We cannot eat or digest adjectives. Our nation may be able to put a man on the moon in a few years, but it still cannot find out how to put a Negro in the legislature of Mississippi (Enthusiastic applause) or put an unemployed worker back on the job. I have nothing against exploration of the moon or the planets, but if we can reach so high that we can challenge the mysteries and dangers of space, surely we can challenge the poverty and discrimination under our feet. (Enthusiastic applause)

And so we must work hard in the days ahead to make the American dream a reality. And we are particularly challenged at this hour to work for strong civil rights legislation. (Applause) I am sorry to say that the administration has compounded confusion. Last year they tragically underestimated the mood of the Negro revolt and did too little. When the stormy events of the summer occurred, a welcome change came when our great president gave the finest speech in civil rights any chief executive has ever delivered, but since then there has been an unseemly haste to retreat and compromise on every important matter. (Applause)

The most appalling example of this retreat concerns the pending civil rights legislation. The subcommittee of the judiciary of the House of Representatives came up with a splendid bill reaching some of the most urgent areas in need. The attorney general [Robert F. Kennedy] immediately attacked the bill as excessively good. He contends it will not attract the support of sufficient Republicans and should be watered down. The first thing to be said is that you don't run until someone is actually chasing you. Why the haste? If this strong bill comes to the floor of the House and some elements require some compromise, changes can then be made. A fighter should keep punching until the bell, and not throw in the towel before the first round. (Enthusiastic applause)

The administration has worked to build a good record in civil rights; it can multiply its achievements and give a sound bill fighting support. Negroes paused this summer because the president expressed his concern, both in his words and bringing forward legislation. They will be betrayed if no bill, or a nothing bill, is the fruit of their confidence in the administration. And so the challenge is before us, to work hard, and through all of the nonviolent means that are at our disposal to go this additional distance and to make the great dream of brotherhood of man a reality.

Just a few days ago in Birmingham, Alabama, the local newspaper said, "When are Negroes going to end these demonstrations and allow things to return to normalcy?" Well, I must say to Birmingham and to others that we all believe in and work for a legitimate, healthy, positive normalcy, but there is normalcy that we will never work to preserve. For we will never forget that it was normalcy in Mississippi that made for the vicious murder of Medgar Evers. It was normalcy in Birmingham, Alabama, that brought about the tragic and ungodly murder of four innocent girls. It is normalcy in Louisiana that prevents Negroes from becoming registered voters. It is normalcy in the villages and hamlets and cities of Georgia that prevents Negroes from staying in motels and hotels.

It is normalcy in the nation that so often takes necessities from the masses to give luxuries to the classes. It is normalcy in the world that makes for the madness of militarism, the self-defeating effect of physical violence, and the poisoning of the atmosphere with nuclear tests. No, we will not return to that kind of normalcy, never will we return to it! (Enthusiastic applause)

We will only reach out for that normalcy in which the brotherhood of man is a reality. We will only reach out for that type of normalcy in which every man will respect the dignity and the worth of human personality. (Applause) We will only reach out for that normalcy when men all over this nation will once more allow Jefferson's words to rise to cosmic proportions—"We hold these truths to be self evident that *all* men are created equal." (Enthusiastic applause) We only will reach out for that normalcy in which justice will roll down like waters and righteousness like a mighty stream. (Applause) We only reach out for that normalcy where *all* of God's children in this nation will be able to walk the earth with dignity and honor! Only that kind of normalcy will we work for. (Enthusiastic applause)

We only reach out for that normalcy where our children will be able to grow up in a better world, and this pending national elegy will be transformed into a creative psalm of brotherhood. This is the normalcy that we work for and when this day comes, we will see a better Birmingham, we will see a better Washington. We will see a better New York, we will see a better America, and figuratively speaking, this will be the day when the morning stars will sing together and the sons of God will shout for joy! (Extended enthusiastic applause)

Photograph courtesy of the Anne Rand Library,
International Longshore and Warehouse Union

As part of his "phase two" campaign against racism, poverty,
and war, King speaks to a gathering of some five hundred union
members at the Labor Leadership Assembly for Peace in Chicago
on November 11, 1967. To King's left, seated, is Congressman John
Conyers (Dem., Michigan).

PART II

Standing at the Crossroads:
Race, Labor, War, and Poverty

I do not come to you as a prophet of doom; I
come to you as one who has accepted the challenge
of our urban ghettos. This is a more difficult
challenge than the one we face in the South,
for we will not be dealing with constitutional
rights; we will be dealing with fundamental
human rights. It is a constitutional right for
a man to be able to vote, but the human right
to a decent house is as categorically imperative
and morally absolute as was that constitutional
right. It is not a constitutional right that men
have jobs, but it is a human right.

—King at the Illinois State Convention AFL-CIO,
Springfield, Illinois, October 7, 1965

X

"The explosion in Watts reminded us all that the northern ghettos are the prisons of forgotten men."

W*hile in the 1960s the industrial unions of the old CIO, such as the packinghouse workers union, began their slow decline due to automation and outsourcing of work by employers, employment expanded for workers of color in the growing service, wholesale, retail, and health-care industries organized by District 65. The union held its national convention with about one thousand delegates in the wake of the voting rights campaign in Selma. That campaign had stirred the nation and brought Walter Reuther and other labor leaders into a mass march from Selma to Montgomery with priests, pastors, students, and civil rights organizers.*

It seemed to be the high tide for the labor–civil rights alliance. But ominous signs of trouble also loomed. Five days after Johnson signed the Voting Rights Act into law, rumors of police brutality set off a massive race riot in the neighborhood of Watts in Los Angeles, California. The riot left millions of dollars of property damage and numerous dead people in its wake. As King had said at the March on Washington, the mass of African Americans still remained stranded as poor people in an affluent society. White reaction subsequently led to defeat of open housing laws in California and the rise of Ronald Reagan and other so-called "white backlash" candidates, causing King to fear that racial polarization would blot out the gains of the freedom movement.

King planned to speak at District 65's convention, but his doctors instructed him to take a break from his grueling schedule. His executive assistant, Andrew Young, went on his behalf and appealed to the union on September 18 to join with King and the SCLC in its coming campaign against entrenched racial-economic discrimination in Chicago, which was to be the opening gun of a new movement to organize in the urban North. Although King did not appear, the speech he would have given survived in the King Papers in Atlanta and provides King's analysis that the freedom movement had moved into a new and more difficult period after the Voting Rights Act. In his assessment, unions had not done nearly enough to fight for equality, and he warned of impending disaster if the movement did not address the causes of the urban rebellions in Watts and elsewhere. King saw a crisis of the labor–civil rights alliance coming and felt that if the unions did not "raise the standard of living of all workers, not merely those under its contracts," the power of organized labor would fade.

—◇◇—

District 65
NEW YORK CITY, SEPTEMBER 18, 1965

Ten years ago in Montgomery, Alabama, the civil rights movement was transformed into a mass movement when it discovered the weapon of mass nonviolent direct action. To illustrate it vividly, we must remember that in the Montgomery Bus Boycott tens of thousands of Negroes united to refrain from patronizing buses. At that point the confrontation was limited because Negroes were not ready to widen their demands nor to exercise their rights more aggressively than in a negative form—boycott. A decade later, after tumultuous conflicts that dotted the South, fifty thousand Negroes with white allies marched through the main thoroughfare of Montgomery to the state capitol and thundered a broad program of demands ranging from employment and social equality to political representation in state offices.

The dramatic growth and maturation of the movement aroused the entire nation and resulted in historic legislative enactments which are altering the face of the South to a degree undreamed of fifteen years ago.

These spectacular developments have, however, masked an important characteristic of the movement: it has not been national in its thrust nor objectives. It has been regional, confined largely to the South. The confrontation of opposing forces met in climactic engagements only in the South. The explosion in Watts reminded us all that the northern ghettos are the prisons of forgotten men.

During the ten years of sparkling progress in the South, the Negro of the North has seen school segregation increase for his children; his tenements, which ten years ago were slums, are now a decade older and less fit for human habitation; his income, which was creeping up in relation to white income, has fallen back; his rate of unemployment has soared to a point in many ghettos where it exceeds the rate of the Depression thirties. The unemployment rate in Watts was a staggering 34 percent.

This retrogression is all the worse because relative progress in the North should have exceeded that in the South or at worst it should have equaled it. In short, the North by now should have been well on its way to dissolution of ghettos; unemployment should have been eliminated, tensions with the police should have been modified or eradicated by long-tested institutions, and interracial relationships should have become a commonplace fact of life.

None of this happened. In fact, the trend moved in the opposite direction.

Many of us had thought that the North would benefit derivatively from the southern struggle. This was another unrealized estimate because northern municipal governments yielded only as little as they were forced to give and tragically the movement in the North was not geared to exert adequate pressure. There was some sincere effort, and the outstanding work of your union is the shining example in that regard. But elsewhere it was not emulated and your example was as isolated as it was splendid.

We are now moving into a new period. The ghettos are not going to remain patient as the South had for decades. A shift in the focus of struggle is going to create tensions in the North which will not abate until root causes are treated.

A missing ingredient in the civil rights struggle as a whole has been the power of the labor movement. Its sporadic and limited support has been welcome, but in relation to its essential strength, labor has made inconsequential contributions to civil rights. As the struggle unfolds in the North, where labor is particularly strong, its omissions will become more evident and more embarrassing. We have talked many times about Negro-labor unity and the multitude of mutual interests we have. Yet this has not vitalized a consistent unity of action.

I believe that we will have to apply to the labor movement some of the lessons we learned in the South to stimulate white moderate support. We had sympathized with the difficulties of moderates who were a timid minority, and for a long period we made no demands. We hoped for some initiatives which never came. A turning point was reached in Birmingham when we were told by a committee of white moderate clergymen to leave and refrain from creating tensions. From jail I wrote an extensive answer charging them and the white church with dereliction of their duties, with moral obtuseness, and in a sense suggested that if the mission of the ministry did not extend to championing justice against flagrant evil, it was no true ministry of God. The effect was far-reaching. Not only did hundreds of publications reprint the "Letter from Birmingham Jail," reaching tens of millions, but some church organizations, in a spirit of self-criticism, reprinted and distributed it. From that point on, a perceptible change occurred in church involvement. While still timorous in the South, it moved forward; in the North it assumed huge proportions, and by the time the events in Selma occurred, the depth of church support was massive. Many now feel the church has been revitalized by the civil rights movement and given a relevancy it so desperately needed.

It may seem harsh to regard labor leadership as merely moderates in a struggle for social justice, but honesty can offer no better definition. At this juncture it must be admitted that church support substantially exceeds labor support. White middle-class support is also well in advance of labor.

To measure up to the tasks ahead in the North we shall have to call on labor to live up to its great traditions. We will have to do it in the spirit of friendship, but without empty flattery that exaggerates a token into a substantial contribution.

If District 65 could give the kind of support to the southern and northern struggle that it has given so consistently through the years then the unions with ten and twenty times your membership and ten and thirty times your resources should be able to follow suit.

Perhaps our fault has been that we have not energetically sought labor's support. We can no longer afford to
make this error because labor is too significant in the
northern cities to be a quiet moderate. The harm in not
welding a true alliance will not alone be to deprive the civil
rights movement of strength. The greater harm will be suffered by the labor movement. It cannot afford to have a
vibrant, dynamic social movement develop which moves
away from it. It is no secret that the ranks of organized
labor are diminishing, that stagnation characterizes it in
both numbers and in influence.

It became in the thirties and forties a great American
institution which reformed countless evils out of industrial
society. It is regrettably not that today. Labor can become
as anemic as the farm bloc if its ranks thin and its importance fades.

The dynamism labor once had is now to be found in
the civil rights movement. We want to affect a unity for a
noble goal that will infuse labor with the vitality that has
made the significant reforms of the fifties and sixties.

In closing I want to express my optimism that our effort
is going to succeed. I know that there are in labor not only
large numbers of genuinely concerned people but among
them many frustrated people. They have not enjoyed being left out of the greatest moral and social crusade of our
times. They have a conscience and a heart, and they will
respond as other decent Americans have when programs
are presented for clear and direct action.

Labor can come out of its apathy only if it fights for a
genuine program for social advancement. It cannot simply follow administration leadership and make routine or
feeble gestures for greater goals. Labor and the civil rights
movement, the unemployed, the aged, and elements of the
church world can unite for a dynamic crusade for a two-
dollar minimum wage covering all who work, not merely

some. A public works program that will level ghettos, create fine housing for the millions now living in fifty- and sixty-year-old tenements, build new schools, hospitals, recreation areas, will do more to abolish poverty than tax cuts that ultimately benefit the middle class and rich.

Negroes need an economic reconstruction of their lives. The labor movement, if it is to remain vital, needs to raise the standard of living of all workers, not merely those under its contracts. As the relative number of workers in unions drops, the strength of labor will fall if it does not become a social force pressing for greater dimensions of wealth for all who labor.

If labor will play this role now, as it did thirty years ago, it will attract every element in the nation that seeks a fuller life. It will share in the respect and affection that is now so generously given the civil rights movement for its social pioneering. It will benefit itself and its allies, and it will reassume its traditional and noble role to make security and brotherhood a reality and not a distant dream.

XI

"Labor cannot stand still long
or it will slip backward."

U nionists attending the Illinois state labor convention
rose to applaud as King entered. Illinois AFL-CIO
president R. G. Soderstrom pledged to work side-by-side
with King and the state's executive board donated $1,500.
The day before, unionists had cheered Peace Corps director Sargent Shriver, who linked the federal war on poverty to the labor movement's historic struggles for social
and economic advance. But Soderstrom's keynote address
to the Illinois convention signified a growing breach between the labor and civil rights movements as he praised
not only President Johnson's war on poverty but also his
military interventions in Cuba, Santo Domingo, and Vietnam. Said Soderstrom, "Labor of Illinois is with him in
his effort to promote freedom and peace throughout the
world and we are going to stay with him." President Johnson had begun a massive escalation of the war that would
soon tear apart not only the country but the labor and
civil rights coalition.

King must have noticed that very few blacks attended
a convention mostly run by older white male career officials. This was not like a meeting of District 65. This
speech is notable for the frankness with which King

addressed the failure of the mainstream unions to fully support the freedom movement or to do anything about or even to comprehend the downward slope for labor created by automation. He offered tough but realistic words about the danger of irrelevancy to unions if they failed to join the social movements of the 1960s or to address the historic problems of racial inequality in American society. King called for a "coalition of conscience" (Walter Reuther's phrase) that could enact full employment and a guaranteed annual income as a way to end poverty and revitalize both unions and the civil rights movement. He hoped that thirty years later people would look back and thank a union and civil rights alliance for pioneering initiatives that ended poverty. Tragically, events would move mostly in the opposite direction.

———◇◇◇———

Illinois State AFL-CIO
SPRINGFIELD, ILLINOIS, OCTOBER 7, 1965

There have always been two groups who have suffered at the hands of the writers of American history—the labor movement and the Negro people. School children learn from their distorted history books even today that our social pioneers and heroes were almost exclusively great presidents, generals, and captains of industry. The contributions of the labor movement are so slighted that they appear as mere accidental phenomena if they receive attention at all.

At the turn of the century, women earned approximately ten cents an hour, and men were fortunate to receive twenty cents an hour. The average workweek was sixty to seventy hours. During the thirties wages were a secondary issue; to have a job at all was the difference between the agony of starvation and a flicker of life. The nation, now so vigorous, reeled and tottered almost to total collapse.

The labor movement was the principal force that transformed misery and despair into hope and progress. Out of its bold struggles, economic and social reform gave birth to unemployment insurance, old-age pensions, government relief for the destitute, and, above all, new wage levels that meant not mere survival but a tolerable life. The captains of industry did not lead this transformation; they resisted it until they were overcome. When in the thirties the wave of union organization crested over the nation, it carried to secure shores not only itself but the whole society.

Civilization began to grow in the economic life of man, and a decent life with a sense of security and dignity became a reality rather than a distant dream.

It is a mark of our intellectual backwardness that these monumental achievements of labor are still only dimly seen, and in all too many circles the term "union" is still synonymous with self-seeking, power hunger, racketeering, and cynical coercion. There have been and still are wrongs in the trade union movement, but its share of credit for triumphant accomplishments is substantially denied in the historical treatment of the nation's progress.

The other group denied credit for its achievements are Negroes. When our nation was struggling to grow in the eighteenth and nineteenth centuries, our place in international commerce was finally secured when cotton became king and the mills of Europe turned on our abundant raw material. That white gold was the product of Negro labor. Even beyond that the very bodies of, then called black gold, built the economies of many nations through the nefarious but immensely profitable slave trade. The clearing of the wilderness, the productivity of the plantations, the building of roads and ports all emerged from the toil of the grossly oppressed Negro, and on these foundations a modern society was built. None of this, however, finds constructive expression in our history books.

It is not a coincidence that the labor movement and the civil rights movement have the same essential origins. Each is a movement that grew out of burning needs of an oppressed poor for security and equality. Each was denied justice by the dominant forces of society and had to win a place in the sun by its own intense struggle and indescribable self-sacrifice.

There were always people to tell labor that it should wait and be patient. The railroad magnate George Baer invoked the divine in these words, "The rights and interests of the laboring man will be protected and cared for, not by labor agitators, but by the Christian men to whom God, in His infinite wisdom, has given control of the property interests of the country." Victor Hugo answered the admonition to wait with a simple equation. He said, "There is always more misery in the lower class than there is humanity in the upper class." Waiting submissively has always meant standing with an empty cup in one hand while the cup of misery overflows in the other hand.

Negroes today are deafened with advice to wait, but they have learned from the experience of labor that to wait is to submit and surrender.

Despite the striking similarities in the origins of the labor movement and the civil rights movement, there are features today that are markedly different. The civil rights movement is organizationally weak, amateurish, and inexperienced. Yet, it has profound moral appeal; it is growing dynamically, and it is introducing basic democratic reforms in our society.

The labor movement on the other hand is organizationally powerful, but it is stagnating and receding as a social force. As the work force has grown substantially in the past twenty years, the ranks of organized labor have remained stationary, and its moral appeal flickers instead of shining as it did in the thirties.

With all its power and experience, labor has been on the defensive for years, beating back efforts to outlaw the closed shop, interference in its internal affairs, and restrictions on organizing activity. It has made wage gains, but its prestige is lower and its influence in government is meager if compared to labor movements of Europe.

Where once the anti-poverty fight was a product of labor's creativity, now the federal government conducts it through agencies essentially apart from labor. The administration determines the form, the tempo, and the style of the anti-poverty program, and receives all the credit for it.

Unfortunately, labor cannot stand still long or it will slip backward. Apart from its loss of influence and leadership, the new technology is undermining its strength. The advance of automation is a destructive hurricane whose winds are sweeping away jobs and work standards.

The new awareness that America in its glittering prosperity still has nearly forty million poor reveals the dangers facing labor and the unfinished tasks it faces. Henry George once said, "Poverty is the open-mouthed, relentless hell which yawns beneath civilized society." Where there are millions of poor, organized labor cannot really be secure.

One of the most publicized areas of the poor, Appalachia, is the huge ghost town of the mining industry overcome by automation and new products. In a few years, steel will have lost one-third of the jobs it had in 1950 as new methods and equipment blot out employment. Food packing, auto and electrical assembly, all industries of this state, are visibly scarred by the consuming flames of automation. The process does not abate because it has socially undesirable consequences, but accelerates because it is invariably profitable to industry to shrink jobs.

Where are the unemployed automation has created? Many, numbering millions, are walking the streets. A large proportion are Negroes who are half hidden in the ghettos. Some have found employment in service industries in low-paid jobs largely unprotected by unions in these unorganized trades. Other millions have retired, some on pensions, some on social security, others on relief.

The tragic and perilous feature common to all is that they have moved from a decent standard of living to an essentially impoverished condition. This process is dangerous for the nation as it reduces purchasing power; it is dangerous for labor as it undermines standards; and it is catastrophic for the Negro who does not even have a toehold on security.

The South is labor's other deep menace. Lower wage rates and improved transportation have magnetically attracted industry. The widespread, deeply rooted Negro poverty in the South weakens the wage scale there for the white as well as the Negro. Beyond that, a low wage structure in the South becomes a heavy pressure on higher wages in the North.

These conditions exist at a time when national wealth and resources are enormous. They exist in a time when labor is still strong, and the civil rights movement is dynamic and expanding. This suggests that the day of structural economic reform is not over but must begin a new birth toward historic heights.

Are we not past the day when layoffs are no longer sufferable? No one any longer suggests that firemen should be paid only when they are putting out fires. They are paid while they are waiting in the firehouse for the call to work. What kind of security do we have when jobs can disappear for periods and families must abruptly sink to lower living standards? Why should older workers be put in competition with younger workers; why should Negro workers and white workers compete for jobs? The answer is a guaranteed annual wage, an adequate minimum wage for all who work without exclusions, and guaranteed employment for all willing to work. These reforms are entirely within our reach—they are entirely practical in a society so rich and productively so abundant. Why should the most affluent and the most powerful nation on earth have unemployment today when most industrial nations of Europe have none at all?

Thirty years ago the young labor movement made government create tens of millions of jobs in a great hurry, and benefitted all of society in the process. Today labor can resume its pioneering role for its own security and at the same time it will dissolve America's most acute and distressing problem—Negro equality and freedom. In creating full employment, the poverty of Negroes will be eliminated; their migrations, which swell ghettos, causing turmoil and suffering, will diminish; their family life will have an economic base on which to find stability and structure. The Negro will be able to shape his new life by his own efforts, freed from the smothering prison of poverty that stifles him generation after generation.

It is a bitter and ironic truth that in today's prosperity, millions of Negroes live in conditions identical with or worse than the Depression thirties. For hundreds of thousands there is no unemployment insurance, no social security, no Medicare, no minimum wage. The laws do not cover their form of employment. For millions of others, there is no employment or under-employment. In some ghettos, the present rate of unemployment is higher than that of the thirties. Education for our children is second class, and in the higher levels, so limited it has no significance as a lever for uplift. The tenements we inhabited thirty years ago, which were old then, are three decades more dilapidated. Discrimination still smothers initiative, and humiliates the daily life of young and old. The progress of the nation has not carried the Negro with it; it has favored a few and bypassed the millions.

I have attempted in this discussion to point up the common interests of labor and the Negro and to sincerely express the respect labor deserves for its creative role in history. Yet, I would be lacking in honesty if I did not point out that the labor movement thirty years ago did more in that period for civil rights than labor is doing today. Thirty years ago labor pioneered in the mass production industries in introducing new equal employment opportunities. It was bold when general support for equality was timid. Today when sentiment for equal rights is powerful, labor is timid. Much of labor has the posture of a moderate, and some of it is reactionary. In this behavior, labor is today not true to its own fine traditions.

The resolution of our differences can be found in the struggle which must be opened to attain fuller security in the affluent society. This is a crusade in which we shall have to be united because the political and economic adversaries we face will not yield except to a greater strength.

I come to you this morning with an appeal to join us in this crusade. At present, the staff of the Southern Christian Leadership Conference is already at work in the city of Chicago. They are busily training the people of the west side to engage in nonviolent action to deliver the rights, dignity, and opportunities to which all people are entitled.

Chicago is our nation's second largest city, and as such it has embodied within it all of the economic and social problems which are inherent in our national metropolitan life. These are the problems which produced the Watts Riot; these are the problems which threaten to destroy our entire nation; these are the problems which breed violence and hatred in our midst.

I am convinced that there are nonviolent solutions to these problems, but our experience in government and throughout this nation has been that nothing will be done until the issues are raised so dramatically that our nation will act. This was the lesson of both Selma and Birmingham, where inhuman conditions had been allowed to exist for hundreds of years. Negroes in the North are not so patient. If a coalition of conscience between the forces of labor, the church, the academic community, and the civil rights movement does not emerge to make these issues inescapably clear and demand their solution, then I am afraid that hostility and violence will breed a crisis of nationwide proportion. Anyone who remembers how quickly the nonviolent movement spread across the South, first in the bus boycotts and then within a year to almost two hundred cities in the sit-ins, will shudder in horror at the thought of violence spreading with similar speed.

I do not come to you as a prophet of doom; I come to you as one who has accepted the challenge of our urban ghettos. This is a more difficult challenge than the one we face in the South, for we will not be dealing with constitutional rights; we will be dealing with fundamental human rights. It is a constitutional right for a man to be able to vote, but the human right to a decent house is as categorically imperative and morally absolute as was that constitutional right. It is not a constitutional right that men have jobs, but it is a human right.

And so I call upon labor as the historic ally of the underprivileged and oppressed to join with us in this present struggle to redeem the soul of America and to revitalize the life of the poor and downtrodden.

The two most dynamic movements that reshaped the nation during the past three decades are the labor and civil rights movements. Our combined strength is potentially enormous. We have not used a fraction of it for our own good or for the needs of society as a whole. If we make the war on poverty a total war; if we seek higher standards for all workers for an enriched life, we have the ability to accomplish it, and our nation has the ability to provide it. If our two movements unite their social pioneering initiative, thirty years from now people will look back on this day and honor those who had the vision to see the full possibilities of modern society and the courage to fight for their realization. On that day, the brotherhood of man, undergirded by economic security, will be a thrilling and creative reality.

XII

Civil Rights at the Crossroads

Probably everyone would agree that the Teamsters union emerged from some of the toughest struggles of the American labor movement—including a general strike in Minneapolis during the Great Depression marked by bloody melees fought with baseball bats and tire irons. Out of brutal struggles came Detroit's James Hoffa and Seattle's Dave Beck, bare-knuckled business unionists willing to use force or bribery to organize workers. They proved much more tenacious and aggressive in organizing workers than most mainstream union leaders and would make alliances with left-wing unions or right-wing bosses and politicians if it benefitted their organizing agenda.

By the 1960s, the Teamsters union had 1.8 million members, making it the largest union in America. Although its white members often practiced discrimination, the Teamsters union rejected the color line and had an anti-discrimination clause in its contracts. By 1964, about two hundred thousand African Americans belonged. When during the Selma to Montgomery march racists murdered Viola Liuzzo, the wife of a Teamster official in Detroit, Hoffa responded by giving King's organization a $25,000 donation. King had spoken to the Teamsters convention *held in Miami Beach in 1961, and received a donation then as well.*

In 1967, the federal government imprisoned Hoffa on corruption charges, and in 1975, he was presumed to be kidnapped and never seen again. King, throughout the 1960s, took care not to be too closely associated with Hoffa or Beck, but he definitely appreciated the role of the union in improving the lives of black workers in the South and across the nation. In his speech to Teamster shop stewards in New York City—presumably, many of them African Americans—King points to the strong participation of black and other workers of color in the union and suggests unions could significantly advance a social movement agenda during a moment of polarization and peril. Although this speech exists in recorded form, further details about the meeting are obscure.

King's reference in this speech to civil rights at the "crossroads" echoes a phrase used by Bayard Rustin—but clearly King was also at that crossroads himself. A month previous, on April 4, 1967, he had come out strongly against the Vietnam War—to the condemnation of civil rights leaders, the mass media, President Johnson's advisors, and many politicians. King had recently weathered a frightening campaign in the summer of 1966. Neo-Nazis and ordinary white homeowners screamed for his blood when he led open housing demonstrations in the nearby suburbs of Chicago, and white supremacists and state police viciously attacked King and other marchers when they tried to conduct a March Against Fear through Mississippi. Paramilitary right and racist organizations as well as the FBI in its "counterintelligence" program targeted King and anyone else in the New Left or the black freedom movement that appeared to have a mass following. But the mass movement also seemed to be splitting apart over King's integrationist goals and nonviolent methods versus a growing emphasis on black power and armed self-defense in the New Left. Within a few months of this speech in New York, Detroit would explode with the most destructive and violent racial rebellion of the 1960s.

As the country polarized, King found himself criticized as too radical by the mainstream and the right, and as not radical enough by the New Left. In this blunt and almost bitter but nonetheless hopeful speech, King analyzes the big divide opening up in American society and tries to bring people back to some sense of a united progressive movement with labor at the forefront. That dream seemed to be shattered a few years later when building trades union officials led hard-hat construction workers to assault anti-war protestors in the streets of New York. Some of King's analysis in this speech appears in his last book, Where Do We Go From Here: Chaos or Community?, *published in the summer of 1967.*

———◇◇◇———

Shop Stewards of Local 815, Teamsters, and the Allied Trades Council
NEW YORK CITY, MAY 2, 1967

There are a great many observers today who feel that the civil rights movement is not at a crossroad but at an impasse. They cry out in despair, "The Negro revolution is a myth—Negroes are worse off than they were ten years ago. The white backlash is proof that the marching, the demonstrating, the blood we shed, the sweat and the toil, were all in vain. The Negro thrust was too weak; and the white resistance was too strong; we have been betrayed and defeated."

Now this is a quotation that I recently read in a national magazine. It is [not] hard to list the grievances still unfilled that make this despair seem all too real. Yet I firmly disagree. When I try to look with perspective at the real historical picture of the last decade I find that I am helped by the experience of labor when it first embarked on mass organization in the 1930s.

There were strikes then curiously different from strikes of today. At present when workers strike or bargain collectively they virtually always win. The question is seldom whether they will gain anything—it is rather how much they will gain. But thirty-five years ago there were strikes where the outcome was not so certain—strikes that meant long weeks and months of intense hunger, conflict, and physical violence, a press and public opinion that depicted the strike as an insurrection. With the settlement of many of these early strikes there was little or nothing added to the pay envelope, little or nothing for job security, and a mountain of debts to pay and harsh memories to forget.

Yet there was one thing that was won—one thing that was fought for as indispensable, one thing for which all the pain and sacrifice was justified: namely, union recognition. It seemed so minuscule a victory that people outside the labor movement scorned it as, in fact, just another defeat. But to those who understood, union recognition meant the real beginning. Union meant strength, and recognition meant the employer's acknowledgment of that strength, and the two meant the opportunity to fight again for further gains with united and multiplied power. As contract followed contract, the pay envelope fattened and fringe benefits and job rights grew to the mature work standards of today. All of these started with winning first union recognition.

I think the biggest gain Negroes have won is that kind of recognition. We might call it not union recognition but human recognition. We have far to go, but like the early labor movement, we have learned that the man who will not fight for his rights has no rights no matter what is written in law or promised by politicians. Labor is respected today; forty years ago it was despised and grossly abused. Negroes are respected today when only yesterday they were scorned, rebuked, and forgotten. Even more important, Negroes respect themselves today and no power exists that can return them to servility and passivity. That is why the white backlash will fail. It may hinder us for a time but it cannot halt us.

What else did we win and what did we not win? What crossroads are we at?

With Selma and the Voting Rights Act one phase of development in the civil rights revolution came to an end. A new phase opened, but few observers realized it or were prepared for its implications. For the vast majority of white Americans, the past decade—the first phase—had been a struggle to give the Negro a degree of decency, not of equality. White America had intended that the Negro should be spared the lash of brutality and coarse degradation, but it had never seriously intended to help him out of poverty, exploitation, or all forms of discrimination. The outraged white citizen had been sincere when he snatched the whips from the southern sheriffs. But when this was to a degree accomplished, the emotions that had momentarily inflamed him melted away. White Americans left the Negro on the ground and in devastating numbers walked off with the aggressor. It appeared that the white segregationist and the ordinary white citizen had more in common with one another than either had with the Negro.

When Negroes looked for the second phase, the realization of equality, they found that many of their white allies had quietly disappeared. The Negroes of America had taken the president, the press, and the pulpit at their word when they spoke in broad terms of freedom and justice. But the absence of brutality and unregenerate evil is not the presence of justice. To stay murder is not the same thing as ordaining brotherhood.

The limited program most of white America had was essentially completed. This is where we are now. White America cannot escape the demand for full equality for economic justice but it would like to, and the task for Negroes and their white allies is to make the nation as a whole face up squarely to the full program.

Negro-white unity was relatively easy to obtain when there was a simple objective of curbing brutality and arrogant humiliation. This brought millions of whites quickly to the side of the Negro, reaching its highest point at Selma. But when the coarse sheriffs were tamed the day of easy unity ended and the day of serious unity started.

The fact that the old superficial unity has had its day and is over, the fact that ugly slums are still with us, that unemployment is so severe for Negroes it resembles the Depression thirties, and the fact that school integration is sluggish and token after more than a decade all make many question if ten years of turbulent struggle was worthwhile.

Let us see if we gained anything, but first let us see what we set out to gain. It is widely overlooked that the Negro revolution was begun in the South, was largely conducted only in the South, and projected programs of reform only for the South. We will inevitably come up with a false result if we look at the North because substantially all of the efforts over the past few years were to support the southern struggle.

The first historic achievement is found in the fact that the movement in the South has profoundly shaken the entire edifice of segregation. This is an accomplishment whose consequences are deeply felt by every southern Negro in his daily life. It is no longer possible to count the number of establishments that are open to Negroes. The persistence of segregation is not the salient fact of southern experience; the proliferating areas in which Negroes move freely is a new advancing truth.

The South was the stronghold of racism. In white migrations through history, from the South to the North and West, racism was carried to poison the rest of the nation. Prejudice, discrimination, and bigotry have been deeply embedded through all the institutions of southern life—political, social, and economic. There could be no possibility of life transforming change anywhere so long as the vast and solid influence of southern segregation remained unchallenged and unhurt. The ten years assault at the roots was fundamental to undermining the system. What distinguished this period from all preceding decades was that it constituted the first frontal attack on racism at its heart.

The second major advance was a multimillion registration of Negroes to vote in both border and deep southern states. There is a Negro electorate in the South that is a formidable force. Let us not be deceived by the raucous voice of a [Governor George] Wallace in Alabama. He still shouts his racism, but hundreds of other white southern officials and candidates no longer rely on the appeal of bigotry. They have learned a new restrained and respectful language, and many of them now meet and confer with Negro leaders in fashioning their campaigns and programs. A decade ago not a single Negro entered the legislative chambers of the South except as a porter or a chauffeur. Today eleven Negroes are members of the Georgia legislature.

The [third] major accomplishment was national legislation. For almost a century, Congress would pass no laws to benefit Negroes. There was no constitution for Negroes. But in a single decade the marching feet of Negroes and their white allies made Congress march to a new tune. In 1957, the first law was passed, in 1960, the second, in 1964, the third, and in 1965, the fourth. A body of federal law finally gave substance to the constitution and though more needs to be done, what was done drove a breach in the solid walls of segregation and let in fresh democratic air and light.

The fourth major accomplishment was the Negro's new visibility. Ten years ago, the Negro was almost invisible to the larger society; the facts of his harsh life were unknown to the majority of the people. In a decade, Negroes made an indifferent and unconcerned nation rise from lethargy and recognize his oppression and struggle with their newly aroused conscience. Today civil rights is a dominating issue in every state, crowding the pages of the press and the daily conversation of white Americans. Negroes made their cause an issue finally to be faced by all Americans because they could no longer escape it by pretending it did not exist.

Finally, Negroes have raised the question of poverty as a responsibility of government and placed a new challenge before society—that no government is moral or ethical or blameless if it cannot eliminate poverty today with the abundance of resources and techniques we possess.

Today Negroes want above all else to abolish poverty in their lives, and in the lives of the white poor. This is the heart of their program. To end humiliation was a start, but to end poverty is a bigger task. It is natural for Negroes to turn to the labor movement because it was the first and pioneer anti-poverty program.

It will not be easy to accomplish this program because white America has had cheap victories up to this point. The limited reforms we won have been obtained at bargain rates for the power structure. There are no expenses involved, no taxes are required for Negroes to share lunch counters, libraries, parks, hotels, and other facilities. Even the more substantial reforms, such as voting rights, required neither large monetary or psychological sacrifice.

The real cost lies ahead. To enable the Negro to catch up, to repair the damage of centuries of denial and oppression, means appropriations to create jobs and job training; it means the outlay of billions for decent housing and equal education.

For this task the nation is frankly not prepared. Words about achieving equality were, and still are, easy to express, but to rise to the responsibility of deeds is harder, and this is where the nation is faltering.

So I would like to put it this way: the civil rights movement is not at a crossroad, it is white America that has reached the crossroad. It has come a part of the way toward its dream of a democratic society, but now many are resisting its fulfillment and wish to stop short to remain a half democracy.

To put it in plain language, many Americans would like to have a nation which is a democracy for white Americans but simultaneously a dictatorship over black Americans. The attempt to hold on to this hopeless and unjust solution and the resistance to the Negro's demand for genuine rights are creating the tensions of today.

White resistance to the necessary next stage of democracy is dividing the nation and creating bitterness and social turmoil.

I want to be very clear that I am not saying we have a pure black-against-white conflict. Tens of millions of white Americans are sincere allies of Negroes. They are allies not only because they cherish decency and justice— they are allies because they know democracy is indivisible. If it can be denied to some because the color of their skin is different, it can be denied to others because they too may be different, whether it be their parent's birthplace, their church, or their station in society.

Another reason that Negroes and so many whites are united against reaction is that Negroes are not the only poor in the nation. There are nearly twice as many white poor as Negro, and therefore the struggle against poverty is not involved solely with color or racial discrimination but with elementary economic justice.

I would now like to briefly suggest a program that I believe is a solution for white and Negro—a solution of the American dilemma, racial and economic.

Up to now we have proceeded from a premise that poverty is a consequence of multiple evils; lack of education restricting job opportunities; poor housing, which stultified home life and suppressed initiative; fragile family relationships, which distorted personality development. The logic of this approach suggested that each of these causes be attacked one by one. Hence a housing program to transform living conditions; improved educational facilities to furnish tools for better job opportunities; and family counseling to create better personal adjustments were designed. In combination, these measures were intended to remove the causes of poverty.

While none of these remedies in itself is unsound, all have a fatal disadvantage. The programs have never proceeded on a coordinated basis or at similar rates of development. Housing measures fluctuated at the whims of legislative bodies. They have been piecemeal. Educational reforms have been even more sluggish and entangled in bureaucratic stalling and economy-dominated decisions. Family assistance stagnated in neglect and then suddenly was discovered to be the central issue on the basis of hasty and superficial studies. At no time has a total, coordinated, and fully adequate program been conceived. As a consequence, fragmentary and spasmodic reforms have failed to reach down to the profoundest needs of the poor.

In addition to the absence of coordination and sufficiency, the programs of the past all have another common failing—they are indirect. Each seeks to solve poverty by first solving something else.

I am now convinced that the simplest approach will prove to be the most revolutionary. The solution to poverty is to abolish it directly by a now widely discussed measure: the guaranteed annual income.

Earlier in this century the proposal would have been greeted with thunderous ridicule and denunciation as destructive of initiative and responsibility. At that time economic status was considered the measure of the individual's abilities and talents. In the simplistic thinking of that day, the absence of worldly goods indicated a want of industrious habits and moral fiber.

We have come a long way in our understanding of human motivation and of the blind operation of our economic system. Now most serious thinkers acknowledge that dislocations in the market operation of our economy and the prevalence of discrimination thrust people into idleness and bind them in constant or frequent unemployment against their will. The poor are less often dismissed from our conscience today by being branded as inferior and incompetent. We also know that no matter how dynamically the economy develops and expands, it does not eliminate all poverty.

We have come to the point where we must make the nonproducer a consumer or we will find ourselves drowning in a sea of consumer goods. We have so energetically mastered production that we now must give attention to distribution. To a degree we have been attacking the problem by increasing purchasing power through higher wage scales and increased social security benefits. But these measures are exercised with restraint and come only as a consequence of organized struggles. Tenacious resistance has caused them to lag behind the rate of increase in our productive capacities. In addition, those at the lowest economic level—the poor white, the Negro, the aged—are traditionally unorganized and have little or no ability to force a growth in their consumer potential. They stagnate or become even poorer in relation to the larger society.

Our emphasis must turn from exclusive attention to putting people to work and shift to enabling people to consume. When they are placed in this position, they can then examine how to use their creative energies for the social good.

The order of priorities is thus changed. If we directly abolish poverty by guaranteeing an income we will have dealt with our primary problem. And we will then see that we can move ahead. Then we will need to be concerned that the potential of the individual is not wasted and help him devise the types of work that enrich the society by enlarging its scope of culture and improving its health, along with other constructive activity. In 1879, Henry George anticipated this state of affairs when he wrote, in *Progress and Poverty*:

> The fact is that the work which improves the condition of mankind, the work which extends knowledge and increases power and enriches literature, and elevates thought, is not done to secure a living. It is not the work of slaves, driven to their task either by the lash of a master or by animal necessities. It is the work of men who perform it for their own sake, and not that they may get more to eat or drink, or wear, or display. In a state of society where want is abolished, work of this sort could be enormously increased.

We are likely to find that the problems of housing and education instead of preceding the elimination of poverty will themselves be affected if poverty is first abolished. The poor transformed into purchasers will do a great deal on their own to alter housing decay. Negroes, who have a double disability, will have a greater effect on discrimination when they have the additional weapon of cash to use in their struggle.

There are two indispensable conditions to ensure that the guaranteed annual income operates as a consistently progressive measure. First, it must be pegged to the median income of society, not to the lowest level of income. To guarantee an income at the floor would simply perpetuate welfare standards and freeze into society poverty conditions. Second, the guaranteed income must not be rigid, but dynamic. It must automatically increase as the total social income grows. Were it permitted to remain static under growth conditions, the recipients would be suffering a relative decline. If periodic reviews disclose the whole national income has risen, then the guaranteed income would have to be adjusted upward by the same percentage. Without these safeguards, a creeping retrogression would occur, nullifying the positive characteristics of security and stability provided by the guaranteed annual income.

The contemporary tendency in our society is to base our distribution on scarcity, which has vanished, and to compress our abundance into the overfed mouths of the middle and upper classes until they gag with superfluity. If democracy is to have breadth of meaning it is necessary to adjust this inequity. It is not only moral but it is also intelligent. We are wasting and degrading human life by clinging to archaic thinking.

The curse of poverty has no justification in our age. It is socially as cruel and blind as the practice of cannibalism at the dawn of civilization, when men ate each other because they had not yet learned to take food from the soil or to consume the abundant animal life around them. The time has come for us to civilize ourselves by the total, direct, and immediate abolition of poverty.

In conclusion, I want to say something about your union because it is not said often enough. The press has had a field day in attacking the Teamsters and many public figures found it advantageous to identify with the attacks on you. In spite of these attacks, you've gone about your significant work and certainly there's one area that I know very well.

The Teamsters union has perhaps the highest percentage of Negroes in its membership of any major union in the country. You did not have to be ordered by courts to take in Negro members; you did not have to be pressured by demonstrations to be fair and decent. You are as subject as any other Americans to prejudice, but you dealt with it as men should. I wish that in this respect other unions, churches, business organizations, schools, and universities would try to learn something from you because in your experiences you can teach some profound democratic lessons to a great many self-righteous critics.

If our nation does not find its way to brotherhood, it is not going to find security and it is not going to find self-respect. I think the leadership for these noble goals is going to come not from the high and mighty but from the ordinary man who, like you, solved problems in work by honestly facing them. Therefore, I hope you will raise your voices and demand to be heard because you have something to say and the future of the nation may well depend upon how carefully it listens to those who had the courage to pioneer and the character to be right.

And may I say that I have not lost faith in the future. In spite of the problems I've talked about and the difficulties ahead, I am absolutely convinced that we are going to achieve our freedom and we are going to win our freedom because however much America strays away from it, the goal of America is freedom.

Abused and scorned though we may be, our destiny is tied up with the destiny of America. Before the Pilgrim fathers landed at Plymouth, we were here. Before Jefferson etched across the pages of history the majestic words of the Declaration of Independence, we were here. Before the beautiful words of the "Star-Spangled Banner" were written, we were here.

And for more than two centuries our forebearers labored here without wages. They made cotton king, they built the homes of their masters in the midst of the most oppressive and humiliating conditions. And yet, out of a bottomless vitality, they continued to grow and develop.

And I say this afternoon that if the inexpressible cruelties of slavery could not stop us, the opposition that we now face, including the so-called white backlash, will surely fail. We are going to win our freedom because both the sacred heritage of our nation and the eternal will of the almighty God are embodied in our echoing demands.

And so I can still sing our freedom song "We Shall Overcome." We shall overcome because the arc of the moral universe is long but it bends toward justice. We shall overcome because Carlyle is right, "No lie can live forever." We shall overcome because William Cullen Bryant is right, "Truth crushed to earth will rise again." We shall overcome because James Russell Lowell is right, "Truth forever on the scaffold, wrong forever on the throne. Yet that scaffold sways the future."

And so with this faith, we will be able to hew out of the mountain of despair a stone of hope. With this faith, we will be able to transform the jangling discords of our nation into a beautiful symphony of brotherhood. Yes, we will be able to speed up the day when all of God's children, black men and white men, Jews and Gentiles, Protestants and Catholics, all over this nation will be able to join hands and sing in the words of the old Negro spiritual, "Free at last, free at last, thank God Almighty we are free at last." Thank you. (Applause)

XIII

Domestic Impact of the War in Vietnam

King spoke on November 11, 1967, at the University of Chicago, as part of a national meeting coordinated by Moe Foner of Local 1199, the health-care workers union, and held in part at the Amalgamated Meat Cutters and Butcher Workmen's union hall on the North Side of Chicago. The Amalgamated's vice president, Abe Feinglass, was one of organized labor's strongest peace advocates. According to the head count at the founding conference of the National Labor Leadership Assembly for Peace, 523 people from fifty unions and thirty-eight states attended. King's speech before this union audience interrupted twenty years of an anti-communist, pro-military consensus within the mainstream union movement.

King had irrevocably taken a stand against President Lyndon B. Johnson's escalating catastrophe in Vietnam on April 4, 1967, at the Riverside Church in New York City—one year to the day before his death. King had thus already issued the most scathing critique of America's foreign policy of the era, in which he condemned America's anti-communist military intervention in the affairs of other nations as imperialism and greed to sustain the *profits of multinational corporations. He carried this analysis further at the labor leadership assembly, which provided the first significant challenge to unbending union support for the war within the AFL-CIO. Its president, George Meany, came from the craft union side of the labor movement that had long supported U.S. wars of intervention. Many unionists saw government military spending as a means to provide jobs during an era of recessions, mechanization, and job loss, and pork chop unionism and reflexive anti-communism and patriotism made workers hesitant to speak against the war.*

But the war also brought inflation, did not fully replace the jobs lost by automation, and consumed investments and taxes that could have gone into creating jobs, health care, and housing. King in this and other speeches increasingly focused on how the war consumed the country's moral and physical resources and undercut efforts to end poverty. When King gave this speech, four hundred and eighty thousand American soldiers fought in Vietnam at a cost of thirty billion dollars a year; over six thousand Americans and perhaps a million Vietnamese had already died in six years of fruitless military escalation. Students, black power and civil rights advocates, women peace leaders, and draft resisters held mass demonstrations and civil disobedience, which King joined after several years of muted criticism. When he did speak out, the New York Times *decried "Dr. King's error," while congressional leaders and many of his allies fiercely condemned him.*

Labor officialdom remained one of the strongest pillars of support for President Johnson's bombing and troop escalations. When students demonstrated against the war at the AFL-CIO's national convention in San Francisco in 1965, Meany denounced them and threw them out. To the New Left, the organized labor movement had become synonymous with conservatism and war by 1967. King's

allies on labor's left led the opposition to AFL-CIO conservatism. Hospital Workers Local 1199, District 65, the
UPWA, the ILWU, the UE, the Mine, Mill and Smelter
Workers union, and other left-led unions had long argued
against escalation in Vietnam. Some key leaders of the
UAW also opposed the war, while Reuther merely called
for negotiations. King had joined with Randolph, Robinson, and the Negro American Labor Council (NALC)
to call for a negotiated settlement in May 1965, only to
be pressured into quieting his stance. Coretta Scott King
meanwhile had denounced the war as "immoral" at a June
Madison Square Garden rally with tens of thousands, and
had long urged her husband to act.

King was the most famous and visible personality attending the National Labor Leadership Assembly for
Peace. Numerous speakers exposed labor's role in supporting America's aggressive wars against national liberation movements in the less developed world. A number
of mainstream unionists rubbed shoulders with anti-war
unionists they had expelled from the labor movement
for their refusal to support an aggressive foreign policy
twenty years earlier. The assembly thus changed the image
many people had of blue-collar workers blindly following
the war and provided a new opening for critical discussion among unionists.

After these five hundred unionists gathered to oppose
the war, however, nine hundred delegates at an AFL-CIO
convention in December reaffirmed their opposition to
"a Communist war of conquest" in Vietnam and gave a
standing ovation to Secretary of State Dean Rusk, an architect of the Vietnam escalation. AFL-CIO convention
participants held a rousing, placard-waving demonstration of continuing support for military victory, while
Meany claimed, with no shred of evidence, that Communists had planned the labor for peace gathering in a secret

meeting in Hanoi, North Vietnam. Yet King and dissident unionists represented a widespread opinion reflected in a Gallup poll in January 1968, that found almost half of rank-and-file union members opposing the war as wrong. Following the upsurge of fighting during the Tet Offensive, 69 percent of Americans polled wanted out of Vietnam. Walter Reuther finally began to move against the war and ultimately pulled the UAW out of the AFL-CIO, which he said was "too fat, too complacent, too far out of touch with the changing times." Like King, he hoped to salvage the possibility of a labor alliance with young people in the civil rights, black power, anti-war, women's liberation, and New Left movements. I have added some of King's introductory parts of this speech found on a tape-recorded version to the edited version of this speech previously available.

---◆◇◆---

National Labor Leadership Assembly for Peace
CHICAGO, ILLINOIS, NOVEMBER II, 1967

Mr. Chairman, distinguished guests, my brothers and sisters of the labor movement, ladies and gentlemen. I need not pause to say how very delighted I am to be here this afternoon and to be some little part of this extremely significant assembly. . . . I don't feel that I come among strangers today for I feel that I'm an honorary member of many labor unions all across the country. (Applause) In fact, I think Cleve Robinson and Dave Livingston of District 65 in New York made me an honorary member a long time ago and I've been a 65er a long time. . . . I want to try to talk very honestly and frankly about this great problem, this great issue that we face as a result of the war in Vietnam. Some of my words may appear to be rather harsh, but they will be as harsh as truth and as gentle as a nonviolent devotee would be. (Laughter)

I want to use as a subject "The Domestic Impact of the War in America." This question is historic because it is an authentic expression of the conscience of the labor movement. As has been said already this afternoon, tens of millions of Americans oppose the war in Vietnam. Never in our history has there been such a passionate, popular resistance to a current war. In addition to the millions upon millions of ordinary people, eminent scholars, distinguished senators, journalists, businessmen, professionals, students, and political leaders at all levels have protested the war and offered alternatives with an amazing tenacity and boldness.

But *one* voice was missing—the loud, clear voice of labor. The absence of that one voice was all the more tragic because it may be the decisive one for tipping the balance toward peace. Labor has been missing. For too long the moral appeal has been flickering, not shining as it did in its dynamic days of growth. This conference, a united expression of varied branches of labor, reaffirms that the trade union movement is part of forward-looking America. (Applause) That no matter what the formal resolutions of higher bodies may be, the troubled conscience of the working people cannot be stilled. This conference speaks for millions. You here today will long be remembered as those who had the courage to speak out and the wisdom to be right.

It is noteworthy that the Labor Party of Great Britain, which, of course, has no responsibility for our actions, nonetheless went on record on October 4 in a formal national resolution calling upon its Labor government to dissociate itself completely from U.S. policy in Vietnam.

(Applause) It urged its government to persuade the United States to end the bombing of North Vietnam immediately, permanently, and unconditionally.

Now what are some of the domestic consequences of the war in Vietnam? It has made the Great Society a myth and replaced it with a troubled and confused society. The war has strengthened domestic reaction. It has given the extreme right, the anti-labor, anti-Negro, and anti-humanistic forces a weapon of spurious patriotism to galvanize its supporters into reaching for power, right up to the White House. It hopes to use national frustration to take control and restore the America of social insecurity and power for the privileged. When a Hollywood performer, lacking distinction even as an actor [Ronald Reagan], can become a leading war-hawk candidate for the presidency, only the irrationalities induced by a war psychosis can explain such a melancholy turn of events. (Applause)

The war in Vietnam has produced a shameful order of priorities in which the decay, squalor, and pollution of the cities are neglected. And even though 70 percent of our population now lives in them, the war has smothered and nearly extinguished the beginnings of progress toward racial justice. The war has created the bizarre spectacle of armed forces of the United States fighting in ghetto streets in America while they are fighting in jungles in Asia. The war has so increased Negro frustration and despair that urban outbreaks are now an ugly feature of the American scene. How can the administration, with quivering anger, denounce the violence of ghetto Negroes when it has given an example of violence in Asia that shocks the world? (Applause)

The users of naval guns, millions of tons of bombs, and revolting napalm cannot speak to Negroes about violence.

Only those who are fighting for peace have the moral authority to lecture on nonviolence. (Applause)

Now I do not want to be misunderstood. I am not equating the so-called Negro violence with the war. The acts of Negroes are infinitely less dangerous and immoral than the deliberate acts of escalation of the war in Vietnam. In fact, the Negroes in the ghetto, goaded and angered by discrimination and neglect, have for the most part deliberately avoided harming persons. They have destroyed property, but even in the grip of rage, the vast majority have vented their anger on inanimate things, not people. If destruction of property is deplorable, what is the word for the use of napalm on people?

What would happen to Negroes if they not only set fires but killed people in the vicinity and explained blandly that some noncombatants had to die as a matter of course? Negroes would be called savages if we were so callous. But for generals it is military tactics.

In the past two months unemployment has increased approximately 15 percent. At this moment tens of thousands of people and anti-poverty programs are being abruptly thrown out of jobs and training programs to search in a diminishing job market for work and survival. It is disgraceful that a Congress that can vote upward of $35 billion a year for a senseless, immoral war in Vietnam cannot vote a weak $2 billion dollars to carry on our all-too-feeble efforts to bind up the wound of our nation's 35 million poor. This is nothing short of a Congress engaging in political guerilla warfare against the defenseless poor of our nation. (Applause)

Thank God we have John Conyers in Congress; I only wish that we had more like him. (Applause)

The inflation of war cuts the pay of the employed, the pension check of the retired, and the savings of almost

everyone. Inflation has stopped creeping and has begun
running. Working people feel the double impact of inflation and unemployment immediately. But Negroes feel its
impact with crushing severity because they live on the mar-
gin in all respects and have no reserve to cushion shock.
There is a great deal of debate about the nation's ability to
maintain war and commit the billions required to attack
poverty. Theoretically, the United States has resources for
both. But an iron logic dictates that we shall never voluntarily do both for two reasons.

First, the majority of the present Congress and the
administration, as distinguished from the majority of
the people, is single-mindedly devoted to the pursuit
of the war. It has been estimated by Senator [Vance]
Hartke that we spend approximately $500,000 to kill a
single enemy soldier in Vietnam. And yet we spend about
$53 for each impoverished American in anti-poverty pro-
grams. Congress appropriates military funds with alacrity
and generosity. It appropriates poverty funds with miserli-
ness and grudging reluctance. The government is emotionally committed to the war. It is emotionally hostile to the
needs of the poor.

Second, the government will resist committing adequate resources for domestic reform because these are
reserves indispensable for a military adventure. The logic
of war requires that a nation deploy its wealth for immediate combat and simultaneously that it maintain substantial
reserves. It will resist any diminishing of its military power
through the draining off of resources for the social good.
This is the inescapable contradiction between war and social progress at home. Military adventures must stultify
domestic progress to ensure the certainty of military success. This is the reason the poor, and particularly Negroes,
have a double stake in peace and international harmony.
This is not to say it is useless to fight for domestic reform,

on the contrary, as people discover in the struggle what is impeding their progress, they comprehend the full and real cost of the war to them in their daily lives.

Another tragic consequence of the war domestically is its destructive effect on the young generation. There cannot be enough sympathy for those who are sent into battle. More and more it is revealed how many of our soldiers cannot understand the purpose of their sacrifice. It is harrowing under any circumstance to kill, but it is psychologically devastating to be forced to kill when one doubts it is right.

Beyond the tragedy at the front, at home the young people are torn with confusions, which tend to explain most of the extremes of their conduct. This generation has never known a severe economic crisis. But it has known something far worse. It is the first generation in American history to experience four wars in twenty-five years— World War II, the Cold War, the Korean War, and the war in Vietnam. It is a generation of wars. It shows the scars in widespread drug consumption, alienation, and the feverish pursuit of sensual pleasures. Yet we cannot call this generation of the young the "Lost Generation." We are the "Lost Generation" because it is we who failed to give them the peaceful society they were promised as the American heritage. (Applause)

And, finally, the whole nation is living in a triple ring of isolation and alienation. The government is isolated from the majority of the people, who want either withdrawal, de-escalation, or honest negotiation. Not what they are now given, steady intensification of the conflict. In addition to the isolation of the government from its people, there is our national isolation in the world. We are without a single significant international ally. Every major nation has avoided active involvement on our side. We are more alone than we have been since the founding of the republic. Lastly, and more ironically, we are isolated from the very people whom we profess to support, the South Vietnamese. In their elections, the pro-war forces received less than one-third of the vote. In the countryside, most of the area of South Vietnam is in the hands of the Vietcong. And the army of South Vietnam has so reduced its role in the fighting it may shortly become the first pacifist army on the warfront. (Laughter and applause)

The war that began with a few thousand Americans as advisors has become almost totally an American war without the consent of the American people. This is an historic isolation that cannot be rationalized by self-righteousness or the revival of unproved dangers of imminent aggression from China. China's incredible internal turmoil suggests it presently threatens only itself. The war domestically has stimulated a profound discussion of the nature of our government. Reported[ly], members of Congress and distinguished political scientists are questioning the trend toward excessive executive power. Senator George McGovern has summed up these views in the following words:

> Congress must never again surrender its power under our constitutional system by permitting an ill-advised, undeclared war of this kind. Our involvement in South Vietnam came about through a series of moves by the executive branch. Each one seemingly restrained, and yet each one setting the stage for a deeper commitment. The complex of administration moves involving the State Department, the CIA, the Pentagon, and various private interests, all of these have played a greater role than has Congress. Congress cannot be proud of its function in the dreary history of this steadily widening war. That function has been one largely of acquiescence, in little understood administrative efforts. The sur-

veillance, the debate, and the dissent since 1965, while courageous and admirable, came too late in the day to head off the foolish course charted off by our policy makers.

"For the future," the senator concluded, "members of Congress and the administration will do well to heed the admonitions of Edmund Burke, distinguished legislator of an earlier day, 'A conscientious man would be cautious how he dealt in blood.'"

The nature of our government is also under scrutiny by the young generation. I have spoken in recent years before hundreds of thousands of young people in their colleges, in the slums, in churches and synagogues. Their comments and questions reflect a sharply rising body of opinion that the inability to influence government to adopt urgent reforms is not a consequence of any superficial ignorance, lethargy, or prejudice, but is systemic. There is more serious discussion today about basic structural change in our society than I can recall over a decade. We have thus far avoided a recrudescence of McCarthyism. It is constantly threatening, but it has not yet been able to gain a secure foothold. It is not for lack of trying by the ubiquitous congressional committees. They are trying to bring down a blanket of intimidation, but a healthy resistance holds them in check. We must constantly be alert to this danger because if its evil is added to all the others, we will have opened the door to other national disasters.

It is worth remembering that there is a strong strain of dissent in the American tradition even in time of war. During the Mexican War, the intellectual elite of the nation, Emerson, Thoreau, and many others, were withering critics of our national policy. In the Congress, a relatively unknown first-term congressman made a scathing address on the floor denouncing that war. The young congressman was Abraham Lincoln of Illinois. At the same time, a young army lieutenant, almost decided to resign his commission to protest the war. His name was Ulysses Grant. So we must keep dissent alive and not allow it to become another casualty of the war in Vietnam. (Applause)

As I move to my conclusion, let me ask you to indulge a personal reference. When I first decided to take a firm stand against the war in Vietnam, I was subjected to the most bitter criticism, by the press, by individuals, and even by some fellow civil rights leaders. There were those who said that I should stay in my place, that I was a civil rights leader and that these two issues did not mix and I should stick with civil rights. Well, I had only one answer for that and it was simply the fact that I have struggled too long and too hard now to get rid of segregation in public accommodations to end up at this point in my life segregating my moral concerns. (Hearty applause)

And I made it very clear that I recognized that justice was indivisible. Injustice anywhere is a threat to justice everywhere. And then there were those who said, "You're hurting the civil rights movement." One spoke to me one day and said, "Now, Dr. King, don't you think you're going to have to agree more with the administration's policy? I understand that your position on Vietnam has hurt the budget of your organization. And many people who respected you in civil rights have lost that respect, and don't you think that you're going to have to agree more with the administration's policy to regain this?" And I had to answer by looking that person into the eye and say, "I'm sorry, sir, but you don't know me. I'm not a consensus leader." (Laughter and applause) "I do not determine what is right and wrong by looking at the budget of my organization or by taking a Gallup poll of the majority opinion." Ultimately, a genuine leader is not a searcher for consensus but a molder of consensus. (Applause) On some positions the coward asks, "Is it safe?" Expediency asks the question, "Is it politic?" Vanity asks the question, "Is it popular?" But conscience asks the question, "Is it right?" And there comes a time when one must take a position that is neither safe nor politic nor popular, but he must take it because conscience tells him it is right! (Applause and cheering)

[In King's written text, he ended with a quote from Socialist Party leader Eugene Debs, spoken before a federal court that sentenced him to ten years in prison for advocating draft resistance during World War I. King used this same quote in his speech to the National Maritime Union, on page 71.]

© Walter P. Reuther Library, Wayne State University

AFSCME Local 1733 sanitation workers on strike in Memphis as National Guard occupied the city following disorders on March 28, 1968. The upheaval forced King to return to Memphis on April 3 with plans to lead a nonviolent mass march.

PART III

Down Jericho Road: The Poor People's Campaign and Memphis Strike

The first question the Levite asked was, "If I stop to help this man, what will happen to me?" But then the Good Samaritan came by. And he reversed the question: "If I do not stop to help this man, what will happen to him?" That's the question before you tonight. . . . If I do not stop to help the sanitation workers, what will happen to them? That's the question.

—King at the sanitation strike mass meeting
in Memphis, April 3, 1968

XIV

"The other America"

K ing gave this speech to Local 1199 National Union of Hospital and Health Care Employees as he traveled the country on behalf of his Poor People's Campaign. This campaign evolved out of his frustrated struggle to attack urban poverty in Chicago in 1966. He first announced it would be a campaign of militant civil disobedience in the nation's capital as a way to attract young African American men away from undisciplined urban riots and to enter them into the politics of nonviolent protest. In this quest, King sought especially to mobilize the unemployed, including workers left behind by deindustrialization in the cities and by mechanization in the countryside. He received very little support from unions and did not seem to have a strategy to get them involved. Most unions at this point knew as little about how to mobilize the unemployed sub-proletariat as the civil rights movement. So King approached the National Welfare Rights Association, through which black women had organized militant protests for improved support for their families, Native American tribes, farm workers led by Cesar Chavez in California, Mexican American nationalists led by Reies Tijerina in New Mexico, and poor whites in Ap-

*palachia. He also tempered the call for civil disobedience
due to congressional fears that they would lead to riots in
the nation's predominantly African American and poor
capital.*

*In trying to mobilize a multiracial movement of the
poor, King branched out into terrain once explored by
the most militant unionists of the 1930s and 1940s. On
March 10, he reached out to one of his strongest allies as
part of a celebratory "Salute to Freedom" organized by the
Local 1199. This New York City–based union consisted
largely of African American, Puerto Rican, and other
workers of color. Its president, Leon Davis, and activities
director, Moe Foner, worked with a multitude of union
officers and people of color active in the union, all of them
fully committed to the civil rights revolution. King had
first supported Local 1199 in a crucial strike in New York
City hospitals in 1959, calling its battle "more than a fight
for union rights . . . it is a fight for human rights and
dignity." As the union doubled and quadrupled its membership and wages during the 1960s, it became a reliable
ally for civil rights unionism and for opposition to war,
racism, and poverty.*

*King introduced this speech by indicating his disap-
pointment with the conservatism of many of the unions.
He contrasted the incredible wealth of the nation with the
horrible poverty of many of its people, including the unemployed but also "people who work full-time jobs for
part-time wages." In this speech, he explains the reasons
for the Poor People's Campaign and his own trajectory
that would lead him to Memphis. (Parts of the typed
copy of this speech in the King Papers in Atlanta are
illegible.)*

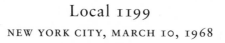

Local 1199

NEW YORK CITY, MARCH 10, 1968

There are times, and I must confess it very honestly as many of us have to confess it as we look at contemporary developments, that I'm often disenchanted with some segments of the power structure of the labor movement. But in these moments of disenchantment, I begin to think of unions like Local 1199 and it gives me renewed courage and vigor to carry on . . . and the feeling that there are *some* unions left that will always maintain the radiant and vibrant idealism that brought the labor movement into being. (Applause) And I would suggest that if all of labor would emulate what you have been doing over the years, our nation would be closer to victory in the fight to eliminate poverty and injustice.

I also believe that if all of labor were to follow your example of mobilizing and involving working people in the campaign to end the war in Vietnam, our nation would be much closer to a swift settlement of that immoral, unjust, and ill-considered war. (Applause)

I know that Leon Davis and Moe Foner have played a decisive role in organizing the Labor Leadership Assembly for Peace, a development that has been a source of great encouragement to all of us engaged in the fight to end the war. I note with pride that your union is sponsoring an all-day fast for peace on March 24 at the Community Church. I sincerely hope that each and every one of you here tonight will personally participate and get others to join you in demonstrating to the nation and the world that Local 1199 represents the authentic conscience of the labor movement. (Applause)

And so for many reasons I'm happy to be here, because

of your fight for justice, your fight for peace, your fight for human decency, and for dignity for every working person.

I don't consider myself a stranger. I've been with 1199 so many times in the past that I consider myself a fellow 1199er. (Applause)

. . . I'm going to really try to be brief, and say a few things about what is happening in our nation and try to say some things about our campaign, our Poor People's Campaign, our campaign for jobs or income which will take place in a few weeks . . . and I want to deal with all of this by using as my subject tonight "The Other America."

And I use this subject because there are literally two Americas. One America is flowing with the milk of prosperity and the honey of equality. That America is the habitat of millions of people who have food and material necessities for their bodies, culture and education for their minds, freedom and human dignity for their spirits. That America is made up of millions of young people who grow up in the sunlight of opportunity.

But as we assemble here tonight, I'm sure that each of us is painfully aware of the fact that there is another America, and that other America has a daily ugliness about it that transforms the buoyancy of hope into the fatigue of despair. In that other America, millions of people find themselves forced to live in inadequate, substandard, and often dilapidated housing conditions. In these conditions they don't have wall-to-wall carpets, but all too often they find themselves living with wall-to-wall rats and roaches. In this other America, thousands, yea, even millions, of young people are forced to attend inadequate, substandard, inferior, quality-less schools, and year after year thousands of young people in this other America finish our high schools reading at an eighth- and a ninth-grade level sometimes. Not because they are dumb, not because they don't have innate intelligence, but because the schools are so inadequate, so overcrowded, so devoid of quality, so segregated, if you will, that the best in these minds can never come out. (Applause)

And probably the most critical problem in the other America is the economic problem. By the millions, people in the other America find themselves perishing on a lonely island of poverty in the midst of a vast ocean of material prosperity. We only need look at the facts, and they tell us something tragic. . . . The fact is that the black man in the United States of America is facing a literal depression. Now you know they don't call it that. When there is massive unemployment in the black community, it's called a social problem. (Applause) But when there is massive unemployment in the white community, it's called a depression. (Laughter and applause) With the black man, it's "welfare," with the whites it's "subsidies." This country has socialism for the rich, rugged individualism for the poor.

Now the fact is that there is a literal depression in the black community. Labor statistics would say that. I mean statistics from the Department of Labor would say that the unemployment rate among Negroes is about 8.8 percent. . . . This does not take under consideration what we would refer to as the discouraged thousands and thousands of people who have lost hope; who have lost motivation; who have had so many doors closed in their faces that they feel defeated; who've come to feel that life is a long and desolate corridor with no exit sign and they've given up. And when you add this, the unemployment rate in the black community would probably be nearer 16 or 18 percent, and when you get to Negro youth, in some cities, the unemployment rate goes as high as 40 percent. Now that's a major depression.

But the problem is not only unemployment. It's under- or sub-employment. People who work full-time jobs for part-time wages. (Applause) Most of the poor people in our country are working every day, but they're making wages so inadequate that they cannot even begin to function in the mainstream of the economic life of the nation. You know where they are working. So often they're working in our hospitals, and all over this country. And I thank God for what your union has done and what you continue to do. I can remember just a few years ago, right here in this city, that hospital workers made wages so inadequate that it was a shame to say to anybody that these people were being paid. (Applause)

But I've been over the country and I know about it. I've been on the picket lines. Hospital workers, whether it's in St. Louis or Cleveland or somewhere else, in Chicago— and I think of the fact that in most instances, in all too many instances, hospital workers are not yet organized. And just think of the low wages in Atlanta, Georgia. I move around as a minister and . . . visit members in the hospitals and . . . they're working every day, working hard, and yet, they are not making enough money to even have adequate food to eat.

Somewhere in life, people of justice and goodwill come to see the dignity of labor. . . . Somewhere they will come to see that person working in the hospital—even if he happens to be a janitor in the hospital—he is in the final analysis as significant as the physician, because if he doesn't do his job, germs can develop, which can be as injurious to the patient as anybody else. (Applause)

We look around and we see thousands and millions of people making inadequate wages every day. Not only do they work in our hospitals, they work in our hotels, they work in our laundries, they work in domestic service, and they find themselves underemployed. You see, no labor is really menial unless you're not getting adequate wages. People are always talking about menial labor.

But if you're getting a good wage . . . that isn't menial labor. What makes it menial is the income, the wages. (Applause)

Now, what we've got to do . . . is to attack the problem of poverty and really mobilize the forces of our country to have an all-out war against poverty, because what we have now is not even a good skirmish against poverty. (Applause) I need not remind you that poverty, the gaps in our society, the gulfs between inordinate superfluous wealth and abject deadening poverty have brought about a great deal of despair, a great deal of tension, a great deal of bitterness. We've seen this bitterness expressed over the last few summers in the violent explosions in our cities.

And the great tragedy is that the nation continues in its national policy to ignore the conditions that brought the riots or the rebellions into being. For in the final analysis, the riot is the language of the unheard. And what is it that America's failed to hear? It's failed to hear that the plight of the Negro poor has worsened over the last few years. It has failed to hear that the promises of justice and freedom have not been met. It has failed to hear that large segments of white society are more concerned about tranquility and the status quo than about justice, humanity, and equality, and it is still true. (Applause) It is still true that these things are being ignored.

Now, every year here about this time our newspapers and our television, and people generally . . . begin to talk about the long hot summer ahead. And what always bothers me about this is that the long hot summer has always been preceded by a long cold winter. (Laughter) And the tragedy is that the nation has failed to use its winters creatively, compassionately . . . and our nation's summers of riots are still caused by our nation's winters of delay. And as long as justice is postponed, as long as there are those in power who fail to address themselves to the problem, we're going to find ourselves sinking into darker nights of social disruption.

Now, I'm concerned about trying to get the nation to use the winter and autumn and the spring and all of this creatively. And this is why we're going to Washington. I wish I had time to talk to you about it in detail tonight. I've been through the ghettos of our nation, been in the Delta of Mississippi. I've been all over and people are frustrated. They're confused, they're bewildered, and they've said that they want a way out of their dilemma. They are angry and many are on the verge, on the brink of despair.

Now, I know that something has to be done. I can't advise them to riot. I don't need to make a long speech tonight. You know my views on nonviolence. And I'm still absolutely convinced that nonviolence, massively organized, powerfully executed, militantly developed, is still the most potent weapon available to the black man in his struggle in the United States of America. (Applause)

The problem with a riot is that it can always be halted by superior force, so I couldn't advise that. On the other hand, I couldn't advise following a path of Martin Luther King just sitting around signing statements, and writing articles condemning the rioters, or engaging in a process of timid supplications for justice. The fact is that freedom is never voluntarily given by the oppressor. (Applause) It must be demanded by the oppressed—that's the long, sometimes tragic and turbulent story of history. And if people who are enslaved sit around and feel that freedom is some kind of lavish dish that will be passed out on a silver platter by the federal government or by the white man while the Negro merely furnishes the appetite, he will never get his freedom. (Applause)

So, I had to sit down with my friends and my associates and think about the people with whom I live and work all over the ghettos of our nation, and I had to try to think up

an alternative to riots on the one hand, and to timid supplications for justice on the other hand. And I have come
to see that it must be a massive movement organizing poor
people in this country, to demand their rights at the seat of
government in Washington, D.C. (Applause)

Now, I said poor people, too, and by that I mean all
poor people. When we go to Washington, we're going to
have black people because black people are poor, but we're
going to also have Puerto Ricans because Puerto Ricans
are poor in the United States of America. We're going to
have Mexican Americans because they are mistreated.
We're going to have Indian Americans because they are
mistreated. (Applause) And for those who will not allow
their prejudice to cause them to blindly support their oppressor, we're going to have Appalachian whites with us in
Washington. (Applause)

We're going there to engage in powerful nonviolent
direct action to demand, to bring into being an attention-
getting dramatic movement, which will make it impossible
for the nation to overlook these demands. Now, they may
not do anything about it. People ask me, "Suppose you
go to Washington and you don't get anything?" You ask
people and you mobilize and you organize, and you don't
get anything. You've been an absolute failure. My only answer is that when you stand up for justice, you can never
fail. (Applause)

The forces that have the power to make a concession
to the forces of justice and truth and right, but who refuse to do it and they follow the path of darkness still, are
the forces that fail. We, as poor people, going to struggle
for justice, can't fail. If there is no response from the federal government, from the Congress, that's the failure, not
those who are struggling for justice. (Applause)

Now, I'm going to rush on and take my seat, but I want
to say that we're going to Washington to demand what

is justly ours. Some years ago, almost two hundred now, our nation signed a huge promissory note, "We hold these truths to be self-evident, that all men are created equal, that they are endowed by their creator with certain un-alienable rights, that among these are life, liberty, and the pursuit of happiness." Oh, what a marvelous creed. Just think about what it says. It didn't say some men; it said all men. It didn't say all white men; it said all men, which includes black men. It didn't say all Gentiles. It said all men, which includes Jews. It didn't say all Protestants, it said all men, which includes Catholics. And I can go right down the line. And then it said something else. That every man has certain basic rights that are neither derived from nor conferred by the state. . . . They are God given.

Now this is what the creed says. Now the problem is America has had a high blood pressure of creeds and an anemia of deeds on the question of justice. (Applause) We're going to Washington to say that if a man does not have a job or an income at that moment, you deprive him of life. You deprive him of liberty. And you deprive him of the pursuit of happiness. We're going to demand that America live up to her promise. We're organizing all over, and as I said, we aren't going begging. We are going to demand justice.

Just let me say to you that I have experiences . . . that leave me a little despondent. I get disturbed sometimes that some of our white brothers and sisters don't understand. A man was on a plane with me the other day and I just didn't feel like arguing. (Laughter) He said, "Now the thing you all need to do is something for yourself." He said all other ethnic groups have come to this country and they had problems, too, just like you all have, but they lifted themselves by their own bootstraps. Then he started telling me about his ethnic background, his parents coming from a country in Europe and how they had lifted themselves by their own bootstraps.

Then he said, "Why don't you Nigras do that?" He couldn't pronounce the word *Negro*, (Laughter) and he meant well, really . . . (Laughter) And I was listening and I didn't mean any harm. As I said I wasn't in an arguing mood. But I said, "Sir, it doesn't help the Negro for unfeeling, insensitive white people to say [this] to the Negro that has been here three hundred, almost three hundred and sixty years now, brought here in chains involuntarily, [while] other people who have been here one hundred or one hundred and fifty years came voluntarily." They've gotten ahead of him [and] I said that doesn't help him to just tell him that. It only deepens his frustration and his sense of nobodyness. And I, then, I looked at him and I said, "Sir, do you recognize that no other ethnic group has been a slave on American soil?" (Applause)

And then I went on to say to him, "But, sir, I've got another thing I want to mention to you. The nation made my color a stigma." And Ossie Davis has said it well. I quoted it in the last book that I wrote. Open *Roget's Thesaurus*. That's a book that gives you all of the synonyms of words. And if you look there for the synonyms for black, they all represent something evil and degrading—smut, dirt, you know, everything. And all of the synonyms for white— pure, chaste . . . (Laughter and applause) So, in our society, you know, a white lie is a little better than a black lie. That's the way, and if somebody goes wrong in a family, you don't call him a white sheep, he's a black sheep, you see. (Laughter) You do something wrong, they don't call it whitemail, [they] call it blackmail. I could go right down the line.

Now, this is a bit of semantics and humorous. But what I'm trying to get over to us is that linguistics, semantics conspired against us to make the black man feel that he was nobody, that he didn't count, made him feel that he was on another level of humanity. That man didn't realize that there was nothing the black man could change because of his disability. He couldn't change his actions. It didn't matter about that. It was a problem growing out of the fact that the nation made his color a stigma.

It is a cruel jest to say to a bootless man that he should lift himself up by his own bootstraps. It is even worse to tell a man to lift himself up by his own bootstraps when somebody is standing on the boot. . . . I had to tell him finally that nobody else in this country has lifted themselves by their own bootstraps alone, so why expect the black man to do it? Nobody else. (Applause) Now, let me illustrate this. And I believe in lifting yourself by your own bootstraps to the extent that that's possible. I think black people and poor people must organize themselves. I think we must mobilize our political and economic power. I really believe in these programs to get your legitimate goals, so don't think I'm not saying that one must not do anything for himself.

But I'm getting at something deeper. I never will forget, and you cannot forget, that in 1863 the black man was freed from the bondages of physical slavery, but he wasn't given any land to make that freedom meaningful. Frederick Douglass had talked about forty acres and a mule and then nothing was done. He was just told, "you're free," and you know it was something like keeping a man in prison for many, many years, and suddenly discovering that he is not guilty of the crime for which he was imprisoned. And then you just go up to him and say, "Now, you're free." But you don't give him any bus fare to get to town. (Laughter) You don't give him any money to get some clothes to put on his back. You don't give him anything to get started in life again. Every code of jurisprudence would rise up against that, but this is what happened.

This is what America did to the black man. We were left illiterate, penniless, just told, "you're free." But . . . the basic thing to be seen is this: at that very moment America, through an act of Congress, was giving away millions of acres of land in the West and the Midwest. Not only did it give the land, which meant that it was willing to undergird its white peasants from Europe with a walk through the economic floor, but it built land-grant colleges to teach them how to farm, provided county agents to further their expertise in farming, and then later provided low interest rates so that they could mechanize their farms. And now, many of these people are being paid millions of dollars in federal subsidies not to farm, and these are the people who are often telling the Negro that he should lift himself by his own bootstraps. (Laughter and applause)

What I'm simply saying is that in this movement in Washington, we are going to demand what is ours and, my friends, the resources are here in America. The question is whether the will is here. And this is the question I'm raising—a question more and more as I move around—something is wrong with the ship of state. It is not moving toward new and more secure shores, but toward old destructive rocks. There's something wrong with the policies, the priorities, and the purposes of our nation now, and we've got to say it in no uncertain terms.

And I simply say to you that I'm afraid that our government is more concerned about winning an unjust war in Vietnam than about winning the war against poverty right here at home. (Applause)

And I close by saying that let all of us assembled here continue to struggle for peace and justice. And, you know, they go together. I know there are those who still think they can be separated. They mention to me all the time, there are those who sincerely feel that. But I answered a man the other day who told me I should stick to civil rights, and not deal with the war thing and the war question in Vietnam. I told him that I had been fighting too long and too hard now against segregated public accommodations to end up segregating my moral concerns. (Applause) And the fact is that justice is indivisible; injustice anywhere is a threat to justice everywhere.

And the other thing is we've got to come to see that however much we're misunderstood or criticized for taking a stand for justice or for peace, we must do it anyway. The arc of the moral universe is long, but it bends toward justice. . . . [King quotes William Cullen Bryant and says, in much the same words that he spoke at the Labor Leadership Assembly for Peace, that he will not abandon his conscience in opposing the Vietnam War simply because his position is not popular.]

And I say that if we will stand and work together, we will bring into being that day when justice will roll down like waters and righteousness like a mighty stream. We will bring into being that day when America will no longer be two nations, but when it will be one nation, indivisible, with liberty and justice for all. Thank you. (Applause)

XV

"All labor has dignity."

While King traveled the country rousing support for the Poor People's Campaign, a civil rights strike broke out in Memphis, Tennessee. On February 12, 1968—President Lincoln's birthday—some thirteen hundred black men walked away from their jobs picking up garbage for the city. Echol Cole, thirty-six, and Robert Walker, thirty, had been crushed to death by a defective packing mechanism on a truck in a city that refused to spend the money to update its equipment, leaving their families with no insurance or even workmen's compensation. The city also sent home workers with no pay when it rained, and made them work extra hours without pay when it didn't. They worked in filth and had nowhere to clean up, suffered terrible injuries, and were treated by whites as "boys," almost as servants during slavery times, all for minimum wages. Working full-time jobs, black sanitation workers lived in poverty and could not adequately feed their families. They felt union rights and recognition, dues check-off, and some degree of job security provided the only solution, but the city's conservative white mayor Henry Loeb refused to even consider it.

On February 23, when the workers tried to reason

with the city council, the police attacked them and their supporters with a crippling, blinding chemical called mace. Most whites in the city united with the mayor against the workers, and the city's commercial media portrayed the strike in an inaccurate, completely biased way. Of all the city's major institutions led by whites, only the AFL-CIO Labor Council took the side of the workers and said they had the right to form unions and the right to strike. The black community, black ministers, and black churches took up the cause of the black workers. Mass meetings every night, daily picket lines and marches, and a boycott of downtown stores led primarily by women put housewives, students, and women and men from various industries and walks of life into the battle for union recognition. The American Federation of State, County and Municipal Employees (AFSCME) had taken up the fight as if the union's life depended upon it, and President Jerry Wurf and top field staff William Lucy, Jesse Epps, and Joe Paisley all had deployed to Memphis. The city tried to kill the strike with replacement workers and police intimidation, and the strike turned into a major new front in the battle for human dignity in the South. As so often happened in such situations, the strikers and their supporters turned to King, the only person who could bring national media attention to their plight.

Except for walking the picket line and battling for the rights of black women strikers at the Scripto pen factory in his hometown of Atlanta in late 1963 and early 1964, King had little experience with a strike. But he had a kinship with the poor from his childhood in the Great Depression and an education in labor issues gained in his many associations with unions. He came to this impasse in Memphis on March 18, and his ability to address worker issues quickly became evident. On that night, strikers and their supporters packed Bishop Charles Mason Temple of the Church of God in Christ, in what the ministerial strike coordinator Reverend James Lawson characterized as a "sardine atmosphere." With no text beyond a few words sketched on paper, King addressed the issues and placed the strike into a wider context. He then pinpointed the issue in Memphis that affected workers everywhere, particularly those in the service economy and in municipal jobs. "You are reminding the nation that it is a crime for people to live in this rich nation and receive starvation wages. . . . It is criminal to have people working on a full-time basis and a full-time job getting part-time income." In a few words, King added union rights for the working poor to his campaign on behalf of the unemployed in both the cities and the newly mechanized cotton country. Memphis thus became the first real front of struggle in the Poor People's Campaign.

As King made his points methodically, members of his audience constantly added their voices in a call-and-response, and King began to preach and build up a head of steam. Toward the end of his oration and looking for a resolution to the issues he had sketched and the emotional climax he had reached, King spontaneously called for a general strike. That is, all the workers, including teachers, students, domestic workers, commercial cleaning people, factory and city workers, would take a day off. This proposal drew great shouts of recognition from his audience. People laughed and cried out, "Yeah, yeah, yeah!" with some of them shooting their fists into the air. It was pure bedlam for several minutes. The reason for this overwhelming response was simple: African American women and men did 80 percent of the low-wage labor in the city. Everyone in King's audience knew that if black workers, teachers, and students in Memphis all took a day off from work, they could shut the city down. King called on his audience to do exactly that to force the city of

Memphis to negotiate a fair agreement with the sanitation union.

General strikes have occurred only rarely in American history and nonviolent direct action on such a scale would have marked a turning point in the trajectory of the black freedom struggles of the 1960s. This looked like the beginning of a new kind of movement, in which workers and the community joined hands in a massive civil rights strike. "You are highlighting the economic issue," said King. "You are going beyond purely civil rights to questions of human rights. That is a distinction." Memphis provided the potential starting point in which a "phase one" freedom movement for equal political and constitutional rights would be followed with a "phase two" for what King called "economic equality."

—◇◇◇—

American Federation of State, County and Municipal Employees (AFSCME)

MEMPHIS, TENNESSEE, MARCH 18, 1968

(Applause) My dear friend James Lawson and to all of these dedicated and distinguished ministers of the gospel assembled here tonight, and to all of the sanitation workers and their families and to all of my brothers and sisters—I need not pause to say how very delighted I am to be in Memphis tonight, and to see you here in such large and enthusiastic numbers.

As I came in tonight, I turned around and said to Ralph Abernathy, "They really have a great movement here in Memphis." (Applause) You are demonstrating something here that needs to be demonstrated all over our country. (That's right) You are demonstrating that we can stick together (Applause) and you are demonstrating that we are all tied in a single garment of destiny, and that if one black person suffers, if one black person is down, we are all down. (Applause) I've always said that if we are to solve the tremendous problems that we face we are going to have to unite beyond the religious line, and I'm so happy to know that you have done that in this movement in a supportive role. We have Baptists, Methodists, Presbyterians, Episcopalians, members of the Church of God in Christ, and members of the Church of Christ in God, we are all together, (Applause) and all of the other denominations and religious bodies that I have not mentioned.

But there is another great need, and that is to unite beyond class lines. The Negro "haves" must join hands with the Negro "have-nots." (Applause) And armed with compassionate traveler checks, they must journey into that other country of their brother's denial and hurt and exploitation. (Applause) This is what you have done. You've revealed here that you recognize that the no D is as significant as the PhD, and the man who has been to no-house is as significant as the man who has been to Morehouse. (Applause) And I just want to commend you.

It's been a long time since I've been in a situation like this and this lets me know that we are ready for action. (Loud applause) So I come to commend you and I come also to say to you that in this struggle you have the absolute support, and that means financial support also, of the Southern Christian Leadership Conference. (Applause)

You are doing many things here in this struggle. You are demanding that this city will respect the dignity of labor. So often we overlook the work and the significance of those who are not in professional jobs, (Yeah) of those who are not in the so-called big jobs. But let me say to you tonight, that whenever you are engaged in work that serves humanity and is for the building of humanity, it has dignity, and it has worth. (Applause) One day our

society must come to see this. One day our society will
come to respect the sanitation worker if it is to survive, for
the person who picks up our garbage, in the final analysis,
is as significant as the physician, for if he doesn't do his
job, diseases are rampant. (Applause) All labor (All labor)
has dignity. (Yes!)

But you are doing another thing. You are reminding,
not only Memphis, but you are reminding the nation that
it is a crime for people to live in this rich nation and receive
starvation wages. (Applause) And I need not remind you
that this is our plight as a people all over America. The
vast majority of Negroes in our country are still perishing
on a lonely island of poverty in the midst of a vast ocean of
material prosperity. (Applause) My friends, we are living
as a people in a literal depression. Now you know when
there is mass unemployment and underemployment in the
black community they call it a social problem. When there
is mass unemployment and underemployment in the white
community they call it a depression. (Applause) But we
find ourselves living in a literal depression, all over this
country as a people.

Now the problem is not only unemployment. Do
you know that most of the poor people in our country
are working every day? (Applause) And they are making
wages so low that they cannot begin to function in the
mainstream of the economic life of our nation. (That's
right) These are facts which must be seen, and it is criminal to have people working on a full-time basis and a full-
time job getting part-time income. (Applause) You are here
tonight to demand that Memphis will do something about
the conditions that our brothers face as they work day in
and day out for the well-being of the total community. You
are here to demand that Memphis will see the poor.

You know Jesus reminded us in a magnificent parable
one day that a man went to hell because he didn't see the

poor. His name was Dives. (Yeah, right!) And there was a man by the name of Lazarus who came daily to his gate in need of the basic necessities of life, (Yeah!) and Dives didn't do anything about it. And he ended up going to hell. There is nothing in that parable which says that Dives went to hell because he was rich. Jesus never made a universal indictment against all wealth. It is true that one day a rich young ruler came to Him talking about eternal life, and He advised him to sell all, but in that instance Jesus was prescribing individual surgery, not setting forth a universal diagnosis. (That's right)

If you will go on and read that parable in all of its dimensions and its symbolism you will remember that a conversation took place between heaven and hell. (Yeah) And on the other end of that long-distance call between heaven and hell was Abraham in heaven (Yeah!) talking to Dives in hell. It wasn't a millionaire in hell talking with a poor man in heaven, it was a little millionaire in hell talking with a multimillionaire in heaven. (Applause and cheers) Dives didn't go to hell because he was rich. His wealth was his opportunity to bridge the gulf that separated him from his brother Lazarus. Dives went to hell because he passed by Lazarus every day, but he never really saw him. (Applause) Dives went to hell because he allowed Lazarus to become invisible. Dives went to hell because he allowed the means by which he lived to outdistance the ends for which he lived. Dives went to hell because he maximized the minimum and minimized the maximum. (Long applause) Dives finally went to hell because he sought to be a conscientious objector in the war against poverty. (Applause)

And I come by here to say that America, too, is going to hell if she doesn't use her wealth. (Cheers and applause) If America does not use her vast resources of wealth to end poverty and make it possible for all of God's children to have the basic necessities of life, she, too, will go to hell. And I will hear America through her historians, years and generations to come, saying, "We built gigantic buildings to kiss the skies. We built gargantuan bridges to span the seas. Through our spaceships we were able to carve highways through the stratosphere. Through our airplanes we are able to dwarf distance and place time in chains. Through our submarines we were able to penetrate oceanic depths."

It seems that I can hear the God of the universe saying, "Even though you have done all of that, I was hungry and you fed me not, (Applause and cheers) I was naked and you clothed me not. (Go ahead. Talk to us) The children of my sons and daughters were in need of economic security and you didn't provide it for them. (Applause) And so you cannot enter the kingdom of greatness." This may well be the indictment on America. And that same voice says in Memphis to the mayor, (Yeah!) to the power structure, "If you do it unto the least of these of my children you do it unto me." (Loud applause)

Now you are doing something else here. You are highlighting the economic issue. You are going beyond purely civil rights to questions of human rights. That is a distinction.

We've fought the civil rights battle over the years. We've done many electrifying things. Montgomery, Alabama, in 1956, fifty thousand black men and women decided that it was ultimately more honorable to walk the streets in dignity than to ride segregated buses in humiliation. (Applause) Fifty thousand strong, we substituted tired feet for tired souls. We walked the streets of that city for 381 days until the sagging walls of bus segregation were finally crushed by the battering rams of the forces of justice. (Applause) In 1960, by the thousands in this city and practically every city across the South, students and even adults started sitting in at segregated lunch counters. As they sat there, they were not only sitting down, but they were in reality standing up for the best in the American dream (Yeah) and carrying the whole nation back to those great wells of democracy, which were dug deep by the founding fathers in the formulation of the Constitution and the Declaration of Independence.

In 1961, we took a ride for freedom and brought an end to segregation in interstate travel. In 1963, we went to Birmingham, said, "We don't have a right, we don't have access to public accommodations." Bull Connor came with his dogs and he did use them. Bull Connor came with his fire hoses and he did use them. What he didn't realize was that the black people of Birmingham at that time had a fire that no water could put out. (Loud applause) We stayed there and worked until we literally subpoenaed the conscience of a large segment of the nation, to appear before the judgment seat of morality on the whole question of civil rights. And then in 1965 we went to Selma. We said, "We don't have the right to vote." And we stayed there, we walked the highways of Alabama until the nation was aroused, and we finally got a voting rights bill.

Now all of these were great movements. They did a great deal to end legal segregation and guarantee the right to vote. With Selma and the voting rights bill one era of our struggle came to a close and a new era came into being. Now our struggle is for genuine equality, which means economic equality. For we know now that it isn't enough to integrate lunch counters. What does it profit a man to be able to eat at an integrated lunch counter if he doesn't earn enough money to buy a hamburger and a cup of coffee? (Applause) What does it profit a man to be able to eat at the swankiest integrated restaurant when he doesn't earn enough money to take his wife out to dine? (Applause) What does it profit one to have access to the hotels of our city and the motels of our highway when we don't earn enough money to take our family on a vacation? (Applause) What does it profit one to be able to attend an integrated school when he doesn't earn enough money to buy his children school clothes? (Applause)

And so we assemble here tonight, and you have assembled for more than thirty days now to say, "We are tired. We are tired of being at the bottom. (Yes) We are tired of being trampled over by the iron feet of oppression. We are tired of our children having to attend overcrowded, inferior, quality-less schools. (Applause) We are tired of having to live in dilapidated substandard housing conditions (Applause) where we don't have wall-to-wall carpets but so often we end up with wall-to-wall rats and roaches. (Applause and cheers) We are tired of smothering in an airtight cage of poverty in the midst of an affluent society. We are tired of walking the streets in search for jobs that do not exist. (Applause) We are tired of working our hands off and laboring every day and not even making a wage adequate to get the basic necessities of life. (Applause) We are tired of our men being emasculated so that our wives and our daughters have to go out and work in the white lady's kitchen, (Applause) leaving us unable to be with our children and give them the time and the attention that they need. We are tired." (Cheers)

And so in Memphis we have begun. We are saying, "*Now is the time.*" Get the word across to everybody in power in this time in this town that now is the time to make real the promises of democracy. Now is the time (Applause) to make an adequate income a reality for all of God's children. Now is the time (Applause) for city hall to take a position for that which is just and honest. Now is the time (Applause) for justice to roll down like water and righteousness like a mighty stream. *Now is the time.* (Cheers)

Now let me say a word to those of you who are on strike. You have been out now for a number of days, but don't despair. (Oh, no) Nothing worthwhile is gained without sacrifice. (Applause) The thing for you to do is stay together, and say to everybody in this community that you are going to stick it out to the end until every demand is met, and that you are gonna say, "We ain't gonna let nobody turn us around." (Cheers and loud applause) Let it be known everywhere that along with wages and all of the other securities that you are struggling for, you are also struggling for the right to organize and be recognized. (Applause)

We can all get more together than we can apart; we can get more organized together than we can apart. And this is the way we gain power. Power is the ability to achieve purpose, power is the ability to affect change, (Applause) and we need power. What is power? Walter Reuther said once that "power is the ability of a labor union like UAW to make the most powerful corporation in the world—General Motors—say yes when it wants to say no." That's power. (Applause) And I want you to stick it out so that you will be able to make Mayor Loeb and others say yes, even when they want to say no. (Applause and cheers)

Now the other thing is that nothing is gained without pressure. Don't let anybody tell you to go back on the job and paternalistically say, "Now, you are my men and I'm going to do the right thing for you. Just come on back on the job." Don't go back on the job until the demands are met. (Cheers) Never forget that freedom is not something that is voluntarily given by the oppressor. It is something that must be demanded by the oppressed. Freedom is not some lavish dish that the power structure and the white forces in policy-making positions will voluntarily hand out on a silver platter while the Negro merely furnishes the appetite. (Applause) If we are going to get equality, if we are going to get adequate wages, we are going to have to struggle for it.

Now you know what? You may have to escalate the struggle a bit. If they keep refusing, and they will not recognize the union, and will not agree for the check-off for the collection of dues, I tell you what you ought to do, and you are together here enough to do it: in a few days you ought to get together and just have a *general work stoppage* in the city of Memphis. (Thunderous cheers and applause) (Yeah! Yeah! Yeah!)

And you let that day come, and not a Negro in this city will go to any job downtown. When no Negro in domestic service will go to anybody's house or anybody's kitchen. When black students will not go to anybody's school and black teachers . . .

(Cheers, shouts, the recording breaks off.)

[After conferring with his aides, King returned to the microphone briefly to say he would return to Memphis to lead a mass march within a few days.]

XVI

To the Mountaintop: "Let us develop a kind of dangerous unselfishness."

After King's stunning March 18 speech, strike supporters made hurried efforts to bring him back to lead the united labor-community general strike that he had called for. Instead, supernatural forces shut the city down, in the form of a bizarre snowstorm in the South in the middle of spring. Reverend Lawson joked at the time that Mother Nature had fulfilled King's demand for a general strike. When King finally did return to lead a mass protest march through downtown Memphis on March 28, angry youths, probably egged on by police agents, disrupted it, smashing windows and providing police with an excuse to go on a rampage. Mayhem and murder ensued. Some seven hundred people went to the hospital, and police killed an unarmed sixteen-year-old named Larry Payne. The national news media and reactionary congresspeople, baited by secret memos from the FBI spinning the events in Memphis, condemned King for "running" from the march (he had pulled out when it turned violent). Memphis had now put King's Poor People's Campaign trek to D.C. in jeopardy.

King vowed to return to Memphis in his quest to lead a nonviolent march, despite opposition from his staff and *a number of warnings that he would be killed if he did. He warned his parents and his wife that someone had put a price on his head. As he left Atlanta for Memphis, airline officials delayed his flight for an hour as they searched for a bomb after someone phoned in a death threat against him. On the evening of April 3, King gave one of his most dramatic and prophetic speeches. In the middle of a violent thunderstorm, with tornadoes and lightning touching down in the surrounding area, King arrived at Bishop Charles Mason Temple without a script, with a sore throat, and slightly ill. Violent weather prevented many people from coming, but nearly all thirteen hundred of Local 1733's members came, as did some of their strongest strike supporters. To this humble gathering, King poured out his last testament. He looked back through all of human history to this particular moment in time and called on people to appreciate their opportunity to once again change history. King placed the Memphis movement into the context of the long struggle for human freedom, as he had done in his first speech in support of the Montgomery Bus Boycott that had begun in December 1955. And he reviewed his years in the freedom movement since that time with gusto and appreciation.*

In the Poor People's Campaign, King challenged a system that created beggars. In Memphis, King invoked Jesus' parable of the Good Samaritan and asked people to put their own lives at risk to help others: "The question is not, 'If I don't help the sanitation workers, what will happen to me?' The question is, 'If I don't help the sanitation workers, what will happen to them?'" For years, King had called on middle-class people, especially ministers, to join the struggle of the poor, and now he infused that message into his support for the Memphis sanitation strikers. He pressed his point home: "We've got to see it through. And when we have our march, you need to be there. Be concerned about your brother." His message was the union message: "You may not be on strike. But either we go up together, or we go down together."

With the history of the movement for a better world as his guide, King's rhetorical fervor lifted his audience higher and higher, seemingly beyond the bounds of the church in Memphis to the world stage. He finally finished with a promise that "I may not get there with you, but we as a people will get to the promised land" and collapsed into the arms of his supporters. Only those who experienced that remarkable, prophetic speech could really know how that moment in time felt. "There was an overcoming mood, an overcoming spirit in that place," said strike supporter Reverend James Smith. "King was like Moses," striker James Robinson told me. "A lot of that stuff he was talkin' about . . . was gonna come to pass."

In his last speech, King demonstrated a spiritual kinship and connection with the working poor that few could match. Memphis striker Clinton Burrows remembered, "It was just like Jesus would be coming into my life. . . . I was full of joy and determination. Wherever King was, I wanted to be there." At a time of great anxiety, King's speech calmed him. "He got up and spoke about the plans to kill him if he came to Memphis. He made it very clear that he didn't fear any man. That is a good spirit, to not fear any man. If you believe in right, stick with it."

The next day an assassin's bullet felled one of the most remarkable mass movement leaders in history.

King made this speech not to the hundreds of thousands who gathered to hear him say "I have a dream" at the Lincoln Memorial in 1963, but to several thousand people supporting a tumultuous, difficult strike by sanitation workers in Memphis. Those who were there remember King at his most prophetic, a man trying to carve out *a stone of hope from the desperate year of 1968, when it seemed a mountain of despair blocked movements for change.*

―◇◇◇―

AFSCME

MEMPHIS, TENNESSEE, APRIL 3, 1968

Thank you very kindly, my friends. As I listened to Ralph Abernathy in his eloquent and generous introduction and then thought about myself, I wondered who he was talking about. (Laughter) It's always good to have your closest friend and associate to say something good about you. And Ralph is the best friend that I have in the world.

I'm delighted to see each of you here tonight in spite of a storm warning. You reveal that you are determined (Right) to go on anyhow. (Yeah, all right) Something is happening in Memphis, something is happening in our world.

And, you know, if I were standing at the beginning of time, with the possibility of general and panoramic view of the whole of human history up to now, and the Almighty said to me, "Martin Luther King, which age would you like to live in?" I would take my mental flight by Egypt (Yeah), and I would watch God's children in their magnificent trek from the dark dungeons of Egypt through, or rather across, the Red Sea, through the wilderness, on toward the promised land. And in spite of its magnificence, I wouldn't stop there. (All right)

I would move on by Greece and take my mind to Mount Olympus. And I would see Plato, Aristotle, Socrates, Euripides, and Aristophanes assembled around the Parthenon. (Applause) And I would watch them around the Parthenon as they discussed the great and eternal issues of reality.

But I wouldn't stop there. (Oh, yeah) I would go on, even to the great heyday of the Roman Empire. (Yes) And I would see developments around there, through various emperors and leaders. But I wouldn't stop there. (Keep on!)

I would even come up to the day of the Renaissance, and get a quick picture of all that the Renaissance did for the cultural and aesthetic life of man. But I wouldn't stop there. (Yeah) I would even go by the way that the man for whom I am named had his habitat. And I would watch Martin Luther as he tacked his 95 Theses on the door at the church of Wittenberg.

But I wouldn't stop there. (All right) I would come on up even to 1863, and watch a vacillating president by the name of Abraham Lincoln finally come to the conclusion that he had to sign the Emancipation Proclamation. (Yeah) (Applause)

But I wouldn't stop there. I would even come up to the early thirties, and see a man grappling with the problems of the bankruptcy of his nation. And come with an eloquent cry that we have nothing to fear but fear itself. But I wouldn't stop there. (All right) Strangely enough, I would turn to the Almighty and say, "If you allow me to live just a few years in the second half of the twentieth century, I will be happy." (Applause)

Now that's a strange statement to make, because the world is all messed up. The nation is sick. Trouble is in the land. Confusion all around. That's a strange statement. But I know, somehow, that only when it is dark enough can you see the stars. (All right, yes)

And I see God working in this period of the twentieth century in a way that men, in some strange way, are responding. Something is happening in our world. The masses of people are rising up. And wherever they are assembled today, whether they are in Johannesburg, South Africa; Nairobi, Kenya; Accra, Ghana; New York City;

Atlanta, Georgia; Jackson, Mississippi; or Memphis, Tennessee—the cry is always the same—"We want to be free." (Applause)

And another reason that I'm happy to live in this period is that we have been forced to a point where we're going to have to grapple with the problems that men have been trying to grapple with through history, but the demands didn't force them to do it. Survival demands that we grapple with them. (Yes) Men, for years now, have been talking about war and peace. But now, no longer can they just talk about it. It is no longer a choice between violence and nonviolence in this world; it's nonviolence or nonexistence. That is where we are today. (Applause)

And also, in the human rights revolution, if something isn't done, and done and in a hurry, to bring the colored peoples of the world out of their long years of poverty, their long years of hurt and neglect, the whole world is doomed. (All right) (Applause) Now, I'm just happy that God has allowed me to live in this period, to see what is unfolding. And I'm happy that He's allowed me to be in Memphis. (Applause)

I can remember (Applause), I can remember when Negroes were just going around, as Ralph has said so often, scratching where they didn't itch, and laughing when they were not tickled. (Laughter and applause) But that day is all over. (Yeah) (Applause) We mean business now, and we are determined to gain our rightful place in God's world. (Yeah) (Applause)

And that's all this whole thing is about. We aren't engaged in any negative protest and in any negative arguments with anybody. We are saying that we are determined to be men. We are determined to be people. (Yeah) We are saying (Applause) that we are God's children. (Yeah) (Applause) And that if we are God's children we don't have to live like we are forced to live.

Now, what does all of this mean in this great period of history? It means that we've got to stay together. (Yeah) We've got to stay together and maintain unity. You know, whenever Pharaoh wanted to prolong the period of slavery in Egypt, he had a favorite, favorite formula for doing it. What was that? He kept the slaves fighting among themselves. (Applause) But whenever the slaves get together, something happens in Pharaoh's court, and he cannot hold the slaves in slavery. When the slaves get together, that's the beginning of getting out of slavery. (Applause) Now let us maintain unity.

Secondly, let us keep the issues where they are. (Right) The issue is injustice. The issue is the refusal of Memphis to be fair and honest in its dealings with its public servants, who happen to be sanitation workers. (Applause) Now, we've got to keep attention on that. (That's right) That's always the problem with a little violence. You know what happened the other day, and the press dealt only with the window breaking. (That's right) I read the articles. They very seldom got around to mentioning the fact that one thousand three hundred sanitation workers were on strike, and that Memphis is not being fair to them, and that Mayor Loeb is in dire need of a doctor. They didn't get around to that. (Yeah) (Applause)

Now we're going to march again, and we've got to march again (Yeah), in order to put the issue where it is supposed to be. (Yeah) (Applause) And force everybody to see that there are thirteen hundred of God's children here suffering (That's right), sometimes going hungry, going through dark and dreary nights, wondering how this thing is going to come out. That's the issue. (That's right) And we've got to say to the nation: we know how it's coming out. For when people get caught up with that which is right and they are willing to sacrifice for it, there is no stopping point short of victory. (Applause)

We aren't going to let any mace stop us. We are masters in our nonviolent movement in disarming police forces; they don't know what to do. I've seen them so often. I remember in Birmingham, Alabama, when we were in that majestic struggle there we would move out of the 16th Street Baptist Church day after day; by the hundreds we would move out. And Bull Connor would tell them to send the dogs forth and they did come; but we just went before the dogs singing, "Ain't gonna let nobody turn me around." (Applause) Bull Connor next would say, "Turn the fire hoses on." (Yeah) And as I said to you the other night, Bull Connor didn't know history. He knew a kind of physics that somehow didn't relate to the transphysics that we knew about. And that was the fact that there was a certain kind of fire that no water could put out. (Applause) And we went before the fire hoses. (Yeah) We had known water. (All right) If we were Baptist or some other denominations, we had been immersed. If we were Methodist, and some others, we had been sprinkled, but we knew water. (Applause)

That couldn't stop us. And we just went on before the dogs and we would look at them; and we'd go on before the water hoses and we would look at it, and we'd just go on singing, "Over my head I see freedom in the air." (Yeah) (Applause) And then we would be thrown in the paddy wagons, and sometimes we were stacked in there like sardines in a can. (All right) And they would throw us in, and old Bull would say, "Take 'em off," and they did; and we would just go in the paddy wagon singing "We Shall Overcome." (Yeah) And every now and then we'd get in jail, and we'd see the jailers looking through the windows, being moved by our prayers, (Yes) and being moved by our words and our songs. (Yes) And there was a power there which Bull Connor couldn't adjust to. (All right) And so we ended up transforming Bull into a steer, and we won our struggle in Birmingham. (Applause)

Now we've got to go on to Memphis just like that. I call upon you to be with us Monday. (Yes) Now about injunctions: we have an injunction, and we're going into court tomorrow morning (Go ahead) to fight this illegal, unconstitutional injunction. All we say to America is, "Be true to what you said on paper." (Applause)

If I lived in China or even Russia, or any totalitarian country, maybe I could understand the denial of certain basic First Amendment privileges, because they haven't committed themselves to that over there. But somewhere I read of the freedom of assembly. Somewhere I read (Yes) of the freedom of speech. (Yes) Somewhere I read (All right) of the freedom of press. (Yes) Somewhere I read (Yes) that the greatness of America is the right to protest for right. (Applause) And so just as I say, we aren't going to let dogs or water hoses turn us around, we aren't going to let any injunction turn us around. (Applause) We are going on.

We need all of you. And you know what's beautiful to me, is to see all of these ministers of the Gospel. (Amen) It's a marvelous picture. (Yes) Who is it that is supposed to articulate the longings and aspirations of the people more than the preacher? Somehow the preacher must have a kind of fire shut up in his bones, (Yeah) and whenever injustice is around he must tell it. (Yes) Somehow the preacher must be an Amos, and say . . . "Let justice roll down like waters and righteousness like a mighty stream." (Yes) Somehow the preacher must say with Jesus, "The Spirit of the Lord is upon me (Yes), because He hath anointed me to deal with the problems of the poor." (Go ahead!)

And I want to commend the preachers, under the leadership of these noble men: James Lawson, one who has been in this struggle for many years. He's been to jail for struggling; he's been kicked out of Vanderbilt University for this struggling; but he's still going on, fighting for the rights of his people. (Applause) Reverend Ralph Jackson, [Reverend] Billy Kyles; I could just go right on down the list, but time will not permit. But I want to thank them all. And I want you to thank them, because so often, preachers aren't concerned about anything but themselves. (Applause) And I'm always happy to see a relevant ministry.

It's all right to talk about "long white robes over yonder," in all of its symbolism. But ultimately people want some suits and dresses and shoes to wear down here. (Applause) It's all right to talk about "streets flowing with milk and honey," but God has commanded us to be concerned about the slums down here, and his children who can't eat three square meals a day. (Applause) It's all right to talk about the new Jerusalem, but one day, God's preacher must talk about the new New York, the new Atlanta, the new Philadelphia, the new Los Angeles, the new Memphis, Tennessee. (Applause) This is what we have to do.

Now the other thing we'll have to do is this: always anchor our external direct action with the power of economic withdrawal. Now, we are poor people, individually; we are poor when you compare us with white society in America. We are poor. Never stop and forget that collectively, that means all of us together, collectively, we are richer than all the nations in the world, with the exception of nine. Did you ever think about that? After you leave the United States, Soviet Russia, Great Britain, West Germany, France, and I could name the others, the Negro collectively is richer than most nations of the world. We have an annual income of more than thirty billion dollars a year, which is more than all of the exports of the United States, and more than the national budget of Canada. Did you know that? That's power right there, if we know how to pool it. (Yeah) (Applause)

We don't have to argue with anybody. We don't have to curse and go around acting bad with our words. We don't need any bricks and bottles, we don't need any Molotov cocktails. (Yes) We just need to go around to these stores (Yes, sir), and to these massive industries in our country (Amen), and say, "God sent us by here (All right) to say to you that you're not treating His children right. (That's right) And we've come by here to ask you to make the first item on your agenda fair treatment, where God's children are concerned. Now, if you are not prepared to do that, we do have an agenda that we must follow. And our agenda calls for withdrawing economic support from you." (Applause)

And so, as a result of this, we are asking you tonight, to go out and tell your neighbors not to buy Coca-Cola in Memphis. (Yeah) (Applause) Go by and tell them not to buy Sealtest milk. (Yeah) (Applause) Tell them not to buy—what is the other bread?—Wonder Bread. (Applause) And what is the other bread company, Jesse? Tell them not to buy Hart's bread. (Applause) As Jesse Jackson has said, up to now, only the garbage men have been feeling pain. Now we must kind of redistribute the pain. (Applause) We are choosing these companies because they haven't been fair in their hiring policies; and we are choosing them because they can begin the process of saying, they are going to support the needs and the rights of these men who are on strike. And then they can move on downtown and tell Mayor Loeb to do what is right. (That's right, speak) (Applause)

But not only that, we've got to strengthen black institutions. (That's right, yeah) I call upon you to take your money out of the banks downtown and deposit your money in Tri-State Bank. (Yeah) (Applause) We want a "bank-in" movement in Memphis. (Yes) So go by the savings and loan association. I'm not asking you something that we don't do ourselves at SCLC. Judge [Benjamin] Hooks and others will tell you that we have an account here in the savings and loan association from the Southern Christian Leadership Conference. We're just telling you to follow what we're doing. Put your money there. (Applause) You have six or seven black insurance companies here in the city of Memphis. Take out your insurance there. We want to have an "insurance-in." (Applause)

Now these are some practical things that we can do. We begin the process of building a greater economic base. And at the same time, we are putting pressure where it really hurts. (There you go) I ask you to follow through here. (Applause)

Now, let me say as I move to my conclusion that we've got to give ourselves to this struggle until the end. (Amen) Nothing would be more tragic than to stop at this point, in Memphis. We've got to see it through. (Applause) And when we have our march, you need to be there. (Applause) Be concerned about your brother. You may not be on strike. (Yeah) But either we go up together, or we go down together. (Applause)

Let us develop a kind of dangerous unselfishness. One day a man came to Jesus and he wanted to raise some questions about some vital matters of life. At points he wanted to trick Jesus (That's right) and show him that he knew a little more than Jesus knew, and through this throw him off base. [Recording interrupted] . . . Now that question could have easily ended up in a philosophical and theological debate. But Jesus immediately pulled that question from midair and placed it on a dangerous curve between Jerusalem and Jericho. (Yeah)

And he talked about a certain man, who fell among thieves. (Sure) You remember that a Levite (Sure) and a priest passed by on the other side. They didn't stop to help him. And finally a man of another race came by. (Yes, sir)

He got down from his beast, decided not to be compassionate by proxy. But, with him, administered first aid and helped the man in need. Jesus ended up saying, "This was the good man, this was the great man," because he had the capacity to project the "I" into the "thou," and to be concerned about his brother.

Now you know, we use our imagination a great deal to try to determine why the priest and the Levite didn't stop. At times we say they were busy going to a church meeting—an ecclesiastical gathering—and they had to get on down to Jerusalem so they wouldn't be late for their meeting. (Yeah) At other times we would speculate that there was a religious law that one who was engaged in religious ceremonials was not to touch a human body twenty-four hours before the ceremony. (All right) And every now and then we begin to wonder whether maybe they were not going down to Jerusalem, or down to Jericho, rather to organize a "Jericho Road Improvement Association." (Laughter) That's a possibility. Maybe they felt that it was better to deal with the problem from the causal root, rather than to get bogged down with an individual effort. (Laughter)

But I'm going to tell you what my imagination tells me. It's possible that those men were afraid. You see, the Jericho road is a dangerous road. (That's right) I remember when Mrs. King and I were first in Jerusalem. We rented a car and drove from Jerusalem down to Jericho. (Yeah) And as soon as we got on that road, I said to my wife, "I can see why Jesus used this as a setting for his parable." It's a winding, meandering road. (Yes) It's really conducive for ambushing. You start out in Jerusalem, which is about twelve hundred miles—or rather twelve hundred feet above sea level. And by the time you get down to Jericho, fifteen or twenty minutes later, you're about twenty-two hundred feet below sea level. That's a dangerous road. (Yes) In the days of Jesus, it came to be known as the Bloody Pass. And you know, it's possible that the priest and the Levite looked over that man on the ground and wondered if the robbers were still around. (Go ahead) Or it's possible that they felt that the man on the ground was merely faking. (Yeah) And he was acting like he had been robbed and hurt, in order to seize them over there, lure them there for quick and easy seizure. (Oh, yeah)

And so the first question the Levite asked was, "If I stop to help this man, what will happen to me?" (All right) But then the Good Samaritan came by. And he reversed the question: "If I do not stop to help this man, what will happen to him?" That's the question before you tonight. (Yes) Not, "If I stop to help the sanitation workers, what will happen to all of the hours that I usually spend in my office every day and every week as a pastor?" (Yes) The question is not, "If I stop to help this man in need, what will happen to me?" "If I do *not* stop to help the sanitation workers, what will happen to them?" That's the question. (Applause)

Let us rise up tonight with a greater readiness. Let us stand with a greater determination. And let us move on in these powerful days, these days of challenge, to make America what it ought to be. We have an opportunity to make America a better nation. (Amen)

And I want to thank God, once more, for allowing me to be here with you. (Yes, sir) You know, several years ago, I was in New York City autographing the first book that I had written. And while sitting there autographing books, a demented black woman came up. The only question I heard from her was, "Are you Martin Luther King?" And I was looking down writing, and I said yes. And the next minute I felt something beating on my chest. Before I knew it I had been stabbed by this demented woman. I was rushed to Harlem Hospital. It was a dark Saturday afternoon. And that blade had gone through, and the X-rays revealed that the tip of the blade was on the edge of my aorta, the main artery. And once that's punctured, you drown in your own blood—that's the end of you. (Yes, sir)

It came out in the *New York Times* the next morning that if I had sneezed, I would have died. Well, about four days later, they allowed me, after the operation, after my chest had been opened, and the blade had been taken out, to move around in the wheelchair in the hospital. They allowed me to read some of the mail that came in, and from all over the states and the world, kind letters came in. I read a few, but one of them I will never forget. I had received one from the president and the vice president. I've forgotten what those telegrams said. I'd received a visit and a letter from the governor of New York, but I've forgotten what that letter said. (Yes)

But there was another letter (All right) that came from a little girl, a young girl who was a student at the White Plains High School. And I looked at that letter, and I'll never forget it. It said simply, "Dear Dr. King, I am a ninth-grade student at the White Plains High School." She said, "While it should not matter, I would like to mention that I am a white girl. I read in the paper of your misfortune, and of your suffering. And I read that if you had sneezed, you would have died. And I'm simply writing you to say that I'm so happy that you didn't sneeze." (Applause)

And I want to say tonight (Applause), I want to say tonight that I am happy that I didn't sneeze. Because if I had sneezed (All right), I wouldn't have been around here in 1960 (Well), when students all over the South started sitting in at lunch counters. And I knew that as they were sitting in, they were really standing up (Yes, sir) for the best in the American dream and taking the whole nation back to those great wells of democracy which were dug deep by the founding fathers in the Declaration of Independence and the Constitution.

If I had sneezed (Yes), I wouldn't have been around here in 1962, when Negroes in Albany, Georgia, decided to straighten their backs up. And whenever men and women straighten their backs up, they are going somewhere, because a man can't ride your back unless it is bent. If I had sneezed (Applause), if I had sneezed I wouldn't have been here in 1963, when the black people of Birmingham, Alabama, aroused the conscience of this nation, and brought into being the Civil Rights Bill.

If I had sneezed I wouldn't have had a chance later that year, in August, to try to tell America about a dream that I had had. (Yes) If I had sneezed (Applause), I wouldn't have been down in Selma, Alabama, to see the great movement there.

If I had sneezed, I wouldn't have been in Memphis to see a community rally around those brothers and sisters who are suffering. (Yes) I'm so happy that I didn't sneeze.

And . . . it doesn't matter now. (Go ahead) It really doesn't matter what happens now. I left Atlanta this morning, and as we got started on the plane, there were six of us, the pilot said over the public address system, "We are sorry for the delay, but we have Dr. Martin Luther King on the plane. And to be sure that all of the bags were checked, and to be sure that nothing would be wrong with on the plane, we had to check out everything carefully. And we've had the plane protected and guarded all night."

And then I got into Memphis. And some began to say the threats, or talk about the threats that were out. (Yeah) What would happen to me from some of our sick white brothers?

Well, I don't know what will happen now. We've got some difficult days ahead. (Amen) But it really doesn't matter with me now. Because I've been to the mountaintop.

(Yeah) (Explosive applause and shouting) And I don't mind. Like anybody (Applause continues), I would like to live a long life. Longevity has its place. But I'm not concerned about that now. I just want to do God's will. (Yeah) And He's allowed me to go up to the mountain. (Go ahead) And I've looked over (Yes, sir) and I've seen the promised land. (Go ahead) I may not get there with you. (Go ahead) But I want you to know tonight, (Yes) that we as a people will get to the promised land. (Applause) (Go ahead, go ahead) And so I'm happy tonight. I'm not worried about anything. I'm not fearing any man. Mine eyes have seen the glory of the coming of the Lord! . . . (Pandemonium and applause)

Photograph courtesy of the Anne Rand Library,
International Longshore and Warehouse Union

*King speaks to Local 10 of the International Longshore and
Warehouse Union (ILWU) on September 21, 1967, when the local
made him an honorary ILWU member. Members of the union shut
down ports to protest his murder and continued to support King's
unfinished agenda for equality, peace, and labor rights.*

EPILOGUE
KING AND LABOR

In May 1957, as King began his arduous climb to the mountaintop, Bayard Rustin had advised him to bring the American labor movement forthrightly into his struggle for civil and voting rights. Rustin virtually wrote out for King the basic concepts of common grievances, common cause, and common purpose that King employed in his labor speeches. King implemented Rustin's advice when invited to Chicago by the UPWA, but he did not accelerate his drive to enlist unions in the civil rights cause until the AFL-CIO invited him to speak in 1961. By the time he was done, union members had become supporters of the movement, from Montgomery to Memphis, despite often contradictory stands by unions on issues of equal rights, poverty, and war.

In the course of his thirteen years of leadership in the freedom struggle, black workers and civil rights–oriented unions virtually adopted King. The ILWU provided financial support and sent telegrams when King was jailed, and its Local 10 in San Francisco made him an honorary lifetime ILWU member, as did Local 1199 and District 65. Cleophus Williams, an African American who began his four-term presidency of Local 10 of the ILWU in 1968, told researcher Harvey Schwartz of the powerful impact King had upon longshore workers when he came to speak to them on September 21, 1967. They responded enthusiastically to King, but as he connected the issues and spoke about the war and the terrible risks ahead "it was a very quiet, somber atmosphere" and almost as if a spell came over the room, according to Mr. Williams. "Dr. King brought about a real feeling of brotherhood . . . his personality was so strong that anyone who was on the outside came on to the inside of learning things and believing things they didn't care about before." Mr. Williams recalled, "I was happy to be so close to him and be in his presence . . . and I was glad to shake his hand and know that I had come this close to Dr. King, one of the leading personalities of the world."

Upon King's death, members of the ILWU shut down the ports of the San Francisco Bay area for twenty-four hours. In the garment district of New York and in various unionized urban areas around the country, workers spontaneously left work and held rallies and memorials for King. The AFL-CIO sent $20,000 to support the strike in Memphis and funds poured into AFSCME Local 1733 from unions all over the country. In Memphis, 40,000 people marched through the streets in complete silence, led by Coretta Scott King who was accompanied by Harry Belafonte, Jerry Wurf of the AFSCME, Walter Reuther of the UAW, and others, to demand a settlement of the strike. Young people held signs saying HONOR KING: END RACISM, and even members of the street gang the Invaders followed nonviolent discipline. President Lyndon B. Johnson sent his undersecretary of labor to Memphis to force the recalcitrant city government to make a settlement with AFSCME Local 1733, which for a time became the strongest and most influential union in the city.

Working-class and poor black people inside and outside of unions took their own initiative after King's murder: they shut down over 130 cities with fires, looting, and a general uprising. The federal government dispatched more troops to contain an insurrection than at any time since the Civil War. After it was over, many people, not only union members, began to demand a paid holiday to mark Martin Luther King's birthday. District 65 got a holiday memorializing King written into its contracts, with the money workers would have made donated to support human rights activities. The movement for a holiday escalated, taken up by Coretta Scott King, Stevie Wonder, and others.

Today it is the only national holiday commemorating one particular American. Annually, the AFL-CIO holds a national gathering on that day, and various unions and community groups hold memorials, dinners, marches, and educational events. AFSCME commemorates King as virtually a founder of this union's modern-day existence as one of the largest unions in America. The American labor movement and industrial employment have dramatically declined since King's death, and yet working people all over still remember what King said in Memphis: "All labor has dignity."

APPENDIX

A NOTE ON THE SPEECHES

Most of these speeches are located in the King Papers at the Martin Luther King, Jr., Center for Nonviolent Social Change in Atlanta, but researchers may locate them in other archival locations as well. Some have been published by unions as pamphlets or excerpted in union newspapers. At least two of them were previously published in collections of King's speeches.

The existence of all speeches has been verified through historical archives, newspaper articles, and other documentary sources. Newspapers were especially helpful, including the *Chicago Defender*, the *AFL-CIO News*, the *Packinghouse Worker*, *UAW Solidarity*, the ILWU's the *Dispatcher*, the *American Federationist*, the *65er*, *UE News*, and the *RWDSU Record*. Useful documentary sources include the papers of the United Packinghouse Workers Union, Highlander Center, and the National Labor Leadership Assembly for Peace at the Wisconsin Historical Society archives in Madison; the United Automobile Workers and American Federation of State, County and Municipal Employees papers at the Walter P. Reuther Archives of Labor History and Urban Affairs at Wayne State University in Detroit; District 65 records in the Cleveland Robinson Papers of the Robert F. Wagner Labor Archives at New York University; various records in the Memorial Archives at the George Meany National Labor College, Silver Spring, Maryland; the Martin Luther King, Jr., Archive in the Howard Gotlieb Archival Research Center at Boston University; and the Memphis Sanitation Strike papers in the Mississippi Valley Collection at the University of Memphis. The Martin Luther King, Jr., Research and Education Institute at Stanford University reproduces some of these (and other) speeches and related details on its marvelous online research database, http://mlk-kpp01. stanford.edu/. And see the institute's volumes of the Martin Luther King, Jr., papers, published by the University of California Press.

King's speeches were often modified and there may be several different versions in existence. We have taken what appears to be the most accurate version and verified and augmented it where appropriate from other written texts or recorded audio. In some cases we have removed (noted with deletion marks and other notations) extraneous introductions or repetitions of certain stock phrases that have appeared in an earlier speech we have used. Noted below is the text we began with and any other text or audio recording used to augment it.

"A look to the future." Twenty-fifth anniversary of the Highlander Folk School, Monteagle, Tennessee, September 2, 1957. Transcription and audio recording courtesy of the Martin Luther King, Jr., Research and Education Institute (hereafter cited as the King Institute), and verified by the Highlander Center Library, New Market, Tennessee.

"It is a dark day indeed when men cannot work to implement the ideal of brotherhood without being labeled communist." Statement in defense of the UPWA, Atlanta, June 11, 1959, in the King Papers of the Martin Luther King, Jr., Center for Nonviolent Social Change Library and Archives, Atlanta (hereafter cited as the King Papers, Atlanta).

"We, the Negro people and labor . . . inevitably will sow the seeds of liberalism." United Automobile Workers union twenty-fifth convention, Detroit, Michigan, April 27, 1961, in the King Papers, Atlanta, verified in "Side by Side in the Struggle for . . . a Decent Standard of Living," UAW Education Department pamphlet, National Labor

College, George Meany Memorial Archives, Silver Spring, Maryland.

If the Negro Wins, Labor Wins. AFL-CIO Fourth Constitutional Convention, Miami Beach, Florida, December 11, 1961, in *Proceedings of the Fourth Constitutional Convention of the AFL-CIO, Volume I,* December 7–13, 1961, and further verified by an audio recording from the King Institute.

"I am in one of those houses of labor to which I come not to criticize, but to praise." Thirteenth Convention of the United Packinghouse Workers Union, Minneapolis, Minnesota, May 21, 1962, in the King Papers, Atlanta, verified and supplemented by a transcribed UPWA convention proceedings in the UPWA Papers at the Wisconsin Historical Society in Madison, and in the *Packinghouse Worker.* The last few paragraphs of King's speech that are not used in this volume can be found in the convention proceedings, UPWA papers, box 21.

"There are three major social evils . . . the evils of war, the evil of economic injustice, and the evil of racial injustice." Excerpts from the address to the District 65 Convention, September 8, 1962, Laurels Country Club, Monticello, New York. Excerpts in "District 65 Hears a Great Man of Our Time," the *65er* newspaper, September 16, 1962, page 7, courtesy of Professor Lisa Phillips; augmented by a recording of the speech from the District 65 Records, Cleveland Robinson Papers, Robert F. Wagner Labor Archives, Tamiment Library, New York University, courtesy of Meredith Davidson and Laura Helton (hereafter cited as the District 65 Records).

"Industry knows only two types of workers who, in years past, were frequently brought to their jobs in chains." Gandhi Society for Human Rights, National Maritime Union Twenty-fifth Anniversary Dinner, Americana Hotel, New York City, October 23, 1962, in the King

Papers, Atlanta, verified by a printed copy (deleted text can be found here) at the King Institute, and articles in the *Chicago Defender* and other news sources.

"Now is the time to make real the promises of democracy." Detroit March for Civil Rights, Cobo Hall, Detroit, June 23, 1963, in the Walter P. Reuther Archives of Labor History and Urban Affairs at Wayne State University in Detroit, supplemented by a version of the speech in Clayborne Carson and Kris Shepard's *A Call to Conscience: The Landmark Speeches of Dr. Martin Luther King, Jr.* (2001) and in *UAW Solidarity* and articles in the *Detroit News* and *Free Press*.

"The unresolved race question." Thirtieth anniversary of District 65, RWDSU, at Madison Square Garden, New York City, October 23, 1963, transcript courtesy of the King Institute, supplemented by excerpts in a District 65 recording, the District 65 records, and verified in the *65er*, courtesy of researcher Laura Helton.

"The explosion in Watts reminded us all that the northern ghettos are the prisons of forgotten men." District 65, New York City, September 18, 1965, the King papers, Atlanta, and District 65 records, speech copy courtesy of Lisa Phillips, verified by Laura Helton in the *65er*. The speech in the King Papers is dated September 16, but Andrew Young spoke on King's behalf on September 18.

"Labor cannot stand still long or it will slip backward." Illinois State Convention AFL-CIO, Springfield, Illinois, October 7, 1965, text in the King Papers, Atlanta, verified in Illinois State Federation of Labor and Congress of Industrial Organizations Proceedings Eighth Annual Convention, October 4–7, 1965.

Civil Rights at the Crossroads. Shop Stewards of Local 815, Teamsters, and Allied Trades Council, New York City, May 2, 1967, the King Papers, Atlanta, verified and supplemented by a recording from the King Institute.

Domestic Impact of the War in Vietnam. National
Labor Leadership Assembly for Peace Conference, Chicago, November 11, 1967, in the Labor Leadership Assembly for Peace records, Wisconsin Historical Society.
Several versions of the speech exist. We have used audio
and printed texts so that the version presented in this
volume is the most complete.

"The other America." Local 1199 Salute to Freedom,
New York City, March 10, 1968, in the King Papers, Atlanta. The District 65 records' text of the speech is courtesy of Lisa Phillips.

"All labor has dignity." AFSCME mass meeting,
Bishop Charles Mason Temple, Church of God in Christ,
Memphis, March 18, 1968, transcription and tape recording, the Memphis Sanitation Strike files, Mississippi Valley Collection, Ned R. McWherter Library, University of
Memphis, courtesy of Ed Frank. Beacon Press has made
every effort to locate the entire audio and transcript but
was unable to do so.

*To the Mountaintop: "Let us develop a kind of dan-
gerous unselfishness."* AFSCME sanitation strike mass
meeting, Bishop Charles Mason Temple, Memphis, April
3, 1968, transcript and recording both in the King Papers,
Atlanta, verified and augmented by the recording at the
King Institute, and the published version in Carson and
Shepard's *A Call to Conscience: The Landmark Speeches
of Dr. Martin Luther King, Jr.*

ACKNOWLEDGMENTS

I owe a debt of thanks to a number of people who helped bring this volume along. Harvey Schwartz searched the International Longshore and Warehouse Union (ILWU) files for details on King, located photos, and interviewed Mr. Cleophas Williams; Lisa Phillips selflessly provided to me a great deal of her own research on District 65; and Kevin Boyle, Kieran Taylor, Robert Zieger, Otto Olsen, and Susan Englander read parts of the manuscript, provided helpful comments, and aided the editing process. The research and writing of Thomas Jackson, William P. Jones, and the Martin Luther King, Jr., Research and Education Institute, which has published multiple volumes of King's papers, provided critical aid in piecing together the stories relevant to this text. Tenisha Armstrong of the King Institute helped me locate copies of several speeches, and Clayborne Carson offered his guidance on how to proceed with documentary editing. Thomas McCarthy and Heather Young, students at the University of Washington at Tacoma, helped me with research, as did Theresa Mudrock and Suzanne Klinger, extraordinary librarians at the University of Washington, and librarian Susan Williams at Highlander Center in Tennessee. Laura Helton at New York University helped me document King's District 65 speeches. Gayatri Patnaik inspired this project, and she and Joanna Green and numerous others at Beacon Press helped bring King's labor speeches to the public. Much thanks to Patti J. Krueger for her personal support and to the Whiteley Center, and the University of Washington at Tacoma for allowing me the time to work on this project. Andrew Heddon of the Harry Bridges Center for Labor Studies at the University of Washington helped to administer research funds. To all these people and institutions, my thanks. Any mistakes or omissions are my responsibility alone. I hope this volume will help others to launch further investigations into the history and topics contained within it.

INDEX

Abernathy, Ralph, 8, 170, 182, 184

Alabama: Birmingham, xvi, 74, 75, 77–78, 87, 88, 90, 93, 97, 107, 175, 186–87; Montgomery Bus Boycott, xvi, xxvi–xxvii, 8, 23, 74–75, 104–5, 174–75, 180; Selma, 103, 121, 125, 126, 175

Albany (GA), 56, 60, 61–62, 66–67

Allied Trade Council, 121–36

Amalgamated Meat Cutters and Butcher Workmen's Union, 49, 137

American Federation of Labor, xxiii

American Federation of Labor and Congress of Industrial Organizations: Central Intelligence Agency and, xxxiii; civil rights movement and, generally, xxv, 31–35, 38–43, 197; Communism and, xxv–xxvi, 20–21, 32, 48; discrimination and, xxx, 24, 31–35; financial support from, 198; formation of, xxv, 20; holiday honored by, 199; industrialization and, 39, 41; March on Washington and, xv, 34; Memphis Sanitation Strike and, 168; racism in, xxviii, xxx, 31–35; segregation in, 31, 32; speeches to, xxx, 31–45, 48, 49, 111–20; United Packinghouse Work-

ers of America and, 20–21, 31–32, 48; Vietnam War and, 111, 138–39, 139–40

American Federation of State, County and Municipal Employees: financial support for, 198; holiday honored by, 199; Memphis Sanitation Strike and, xvii, xxxiv–xxxv, xxxv, xxxvi, xxxix, 167–78, 179–95

American Federation of Teachers, 32

American Revolutionary War, 91

Amos, 17–18

back-to-Africa movement, 62, 122–23

Baer, George, 114

Beck, Dave, 121, 122

Belafonte, Harry, 198

Berry, Abner, 7

Birmingham (AL): imprisonment in, 107; mass movement in, xvi, 74, 75, 77–78, 87, 88, 90, 186–87; public accommodations in, 175; violence in, 88, 93, 97

black freedom movement: accomplishments of, 81, 174–75, 183–85, 193–94; democracy and, 42–43; desegregation and, 15–16; economic justice and, xvi–xviii, 117–20, 128–34; financial support for, xxvii, 20, 33, 34,

209

"Star Spangled Banner," 135
strikes, 167–78, 179–95, 198
Student Nonviolent Coordinating Committee (SNCC), xv
suffrage. *See* voting
Supreme Court, xxii, 6, 9, 10,
91
Swainson, John B., 74

Taft-Hartley Act, xxiv, 6–7
Teamsters, xxx, 66, 121–36
Thoreau, Henry David, 147
Tijerina, Reies, 153
Till, Emmett, xxvi, 60, 85
Transport Workers Union, 66
Truman, Harry S., xxii, xxiv, 39
truth, 16–17, 30, 44, 135

the unemployed, 153–54
union shop, xxiv, 6–7
United Automobile Workers:
accomplishments of, 25, 26;
Chicago mass movement and,
xxxii; civil rights movement
and, generally, xxvii, 23–30,
34; Communism and, 23;
Congress and, 75; decline
of, 76; discrimination in, 23;
District 65 joins, 56; financial
support from, 75; General
Motors and, 177; March for
Civil Rights and, 74–75;
March on Washington and,
xv, 75; Montgomery Bus
Boycott and, 23, 74–75;
segregation in, 23; speeches
to, xxix, 23–30; Vietnam War
and, xxxiii, 139, 140
United Electrical, Radio and
Machine Workers Union,
xxv, xxviii, xxxviii, 66, 139

United Mine Workers, xxiii
United Nations, 58
United Packinghouse Workers
of America: American Fed-
eration of Labor and Congress
of Industrial Organizations
and, 20–21, 31–32, 48; Chicago mass movement and,
xxxii; civil rights movement
and, generally, xxvi, xxviii,
19–22, 33, 34, 47–54, 197;
Communism and, 20–22, 48;
Congress of Industrial Organizations and, 20; decline of,
49, 103; desegregation and,
20; discrimination and, xxvi,
20, 21–22, 50–51; industrialization and, 49, 51–52; labor
movement and, 20; Mont-
gomery Bus Boycott and,
xxvi–xxvii; Negro American
Labor Council and, 31–32;
racism in, 50–51; segregation
and, 21–22; Southern Christian Leadership Conference
and, 21–22, 47, 50; speeches
to, 19–22, 47–54; Vietnam
War and, 139
U.S. armed forces, xxii
U.S. Congress. *See* Congress
U.S. Supreme Court. *See*
Supreme Court

Vietnam, xxv, xxviii. *See also*
Vietnam War
Vietnam War: American Federation of Labor and Congress
of Industrial Organizations
and, 111, 138–39, 139–40;
civil rights movement and,
148–49, 165–66; Communism